16-18

Civil Liberty

and

Civil Rights

by EDWIN S. NEWMAN, LL.B.

*(A new and updated volume, replacing
Law of Civil Rights and Civil Liberties)*

42711

Oceana Publications, Inc.

Dobbs Ferry, New York

The Legal Almanac Series brings you the law on various subjects in non-technical language. These books do not take the place of your attorney's advice, but they can introduce you to your legal rights and responsibilities.

MANUFACTURED IN THE
UNITED STATES OF AMERICA

TABLE OF CONTENTS

INTRODUCTION

Civil Liberties and Civil Rights

Definition and Distinction

When our founding fathers made us one nation, they had this fear—that a strong central government might overrun the rights of the people. To prevent this, they drew up a list of prohibitions which the federal government was forbidden to do. No religion was to be established; the people were to enjoy freedom of speech, press, assembly and religious worship; a man's life, liberty and property were to be protected against arbitrary action by government. These prohibitions, securing freedom of expression and the protection of personal liberty, were set down in the Bill of Rights, the first ten amendments to the Constitution.

Initially, these prohibitions were directed only against the federal government. The respective states, however, in their own constitutions, adopted similar prohibitions protecting the liberty of the people against arbitrary action by state government. Then, after the Civil War, the Fourteenth Amendment to the Constitution was passed. Under this amendment, no state could deprive any person of life, liberty or property without due process of law. Gradually, this "due process" clause of the Fourteenth Amendment came to include most of the prohibitions of the Bill of Rights, so that the Constitution became complete protection for the people against the action of both state and federal government. These rights, protected by the Bill of Rights and by the Fourteenth Amendment, are known as our "civil liberties."

Specifically, they include the requirement that Church and State be separated; the freedom of speech, press, assembly and religion; protection against double jeopardy; the right not to be a witness against oneself; protection against unreasonable searches and seizures and against excessive fines and punishments; the right to counsel in criminal cases; and the right to trial by jury. Of course, the exercise of these rights is not absolute; nor is the extent of protection always the same regardless of whether a state or the federal government is involved.

It is one thing, however, to protect the people against the government; it is quite another to protect them against themselves. While the founding fathers dealt wisely with the possibility of tyranny by government, it was only through trial and error experience that we came gradually to deal with the problem of the tyranny of the majority.

Under the Constitution, the government could not act to quiet an unpopular viewpoint; but there was little to stand in the way of a mob riding a man out of town because he spoke his mind. Under the Constitution, the government could not act to establish any one religion; yet, there are pages of our history which tell of unpunished burnings of churches, libels and slanders against members of minority religious groups and incitement to violence against them. Under the Constitution, the government could not reduce any American to second class citizenship because of the color of his skin or his racial origin; intolerance, however, created discrimination against colored persons, and in some instances, the outright threat to their lives, liberty and property.

Over the past hundred years, this problem of the protection of the people from one another has come to be dealt with in an increasingly effective and successful way—through a combination of amendments to the federal Constitution, through state and federal legislation, and perhaps, most significantly, through the courts, and in particular, the United States Supreme Court. The rights thus created, designed to protect the equal standing of the individual before his government, but primarily to protect the freedom of the individual against attacks by other persons, are known as our "civil rights."

Chapter One

FREEDOM OF EXPRESSION

I. PROTECTION OF PUBLIC WELFARE

There is no absolute right to express oneself. But it is fair to say that freedom of speech, press, assembly and religion are preferred liberties. To understand how they work, one must understand the underlying philosophy of freedom of expression in a democratic society.

There is a market place of ideas where, like goods, ideas may be bought and sold. This market is governed by free trade. Any idea may be expressed, and it will be driven from the market only by its own failure to win a following.

But, just as law operates to forbid unfair practices in selling goods, so it has the task of protecting the consuming public against these practices in the sale of ideas. Thus, fraud and untruth have never been protected in the name of free speech. Neither the First Amendment nor the Fourteenth Amendment is a defense to prosecution for fraud or to civil or criminal suits for libel or slander. Only truth, or the reasonable belief that what one has said is true, is relevant in defense.

Moreover, utterances that are not part of the expression of an idea are not really "speech" and therefore do not enjoy the protection of the Constitution. Lewd, obscene, insulting or blasphemous utterances, when they are made solely for their own sakes, and not to get across an idea, can be punished by law. In fact, the major issue involved in censorship of books, films and other reading or seeing matter is the point at which the written or spoken word ceases to be the expression of an idea and becomes outright smut.

1

A. Censorship

Indecency, obscenity, lewdness—all are forbidden by the criminal codes of the forty-eight states. The typical state law, for example, provides for fine and imprisonment of a bookseller or publisher of a book or magazine that is "obscene, indecent, impure, or manifestly tends to corrupt the morals of youth." The typical state law likewise provides for fine and imprisonment of a producer or actors of a theatrical production that is "lewd, obscene, indecent, immoral or impure."

The essential question is as to what constitutes being "lewd, obscene, indecent, immoral or impure." The Supreme Court of the United States furnished a definition in the case of *Roth* v. *United States,* decided in 1957. In upholding the conviction of the defendant bookseller, the majority opinion defined "obscene material" as that "which deals with sex in a manner appealing to 'prurient interest'," i.e. material having a tendency to excite lustful thoughts. By further refinement, the material must be "prurient" to the average person, applying contemporary community standards, and must be "prurient" as a whole, rather than in isolated instances. In setting out this definition, Mr. Justice Brennan noted that "sex and obscenity are not synonymous" and that "the portrayal of sex, e.g. in art, literature and scientific works, is not itself sufficient reason to deny material the constitutional protection of freedom of speech and press."

A case like the *Roth case* would seem not to involve an issue of censorship. A book or play makes its way into the market, and if it is thought to be a violation of the obscenity law, criminal prosecution may follow. But censorship comes into the picture because the average bookseller or theatrical producer does not want to risk his own judgment leading him into criminal prosecution under a state obscenity law. Resultant fine and imprisonment would destroy his reputation and put him out of business. He wants to know in advance whether his product is consistent with good morals and decency.

Accordingly, across the country, either the mayor of a

city, or his delegate, or the licensing commissioner, or the police commissioner, or private "decency" organizations or religious organizations undertake, in some instances by law, and in other instances by custom, to censor and to ban—in short, to tell the citizenry what they may read or see and what they may not. As it is applied respectively to theatrical productions, books and magazines, motion pictures, radio and TV, and the mails, here is the way that censorship works.

Theatrical productions

The staging of an "obscene" play leaves the producer and the actors liable to criminal prosecution. The theater in which such a play is housed, moreover, runs the risk of losing its license.

Frequently, actors are willing for prosecution, content in the knowledge that a jury will not convict. Producers and theatre owners, however, with much more to lose in terms of financial investment, are seldom willing to risk prosecution. The mere threat of prosecution is usually sufficient to get them to take a play off the boards, the feelings of the actors notwithstanding.

This means that the real enforcement of a morality code rests not with a jury in a criminal proceeding after a play has been presented, but with an official censor who may ban it in advance of presentation. Such an official dramatic censor operates in Boston. In New York City, the licensing commissioner operates as censor, sometimes, as in the days of Mayor La Guardia, with the vigilant assistance of the mayor. In other cities, the police commissioner is the guardian of public morals.

In this scheme of things, the state laws become almost inoperative. Municipal enforcement by advance censorship becomes the rule.

Books and Magazines

Plays, burlesques and other forms of entertainment have generally been regarded by the courts as not involving the issue of freedom of expression. This has been true despite

3

the fact that it is a very thin line that separates "entertainment" from "exposition of an idea," particularly in the serious play that may deal with sex or morals in an unorthodox way.

Where books and magazines are involved, however, the issue of freedom of press is clearly posed, and advance censorship becomes doubtful. An influential publisher will frequently risk criminal prosecution, knowing that his mass volume business will not suffer too greatly if he goes to bat for a particular book. Moreover, if he wins, the fact that a book has become controversial will establish it as a best seller. For the publisher, the risk of criminal prosecution may be good business.

For the bookseller, however, criminal prosecution presents the same risk encountered by the producer of an "obscene" play. Successful criminal prosecution can put so great a drain on him that he can be put out of business. Accordingly, booksellers have sought some means of advance clearance of books in order to avoid these risks.

Out-and-out censorship of books and publications would violate freedom of press. The law may restrain sale or distribution of certain publications which fall within narrow statutory definitions, but the law may not prevent publication. Accordingly, in many communities, either the District Attorney, the police, private organizations concerned about decency, the booksellers themselves or all four collaborate to determine in advance what publications shall be "prohibited." The word, "prohibited," is used advisedly since a bookseller who violates the informal ban would leave himself wide open to criminal prosecution. There is, of course, no appeal to the courts from the decision of informal censors.

A law passed in Massachusetts, at the instigation of the booksellers themselves, attempts to provide for official censorship, yet within the bounds of the Constitution. Instead of a criminal prosecution against a book seller, the Massachusetts law affords the alternative of a civil proceeding against the book. Since such a suit asks a court injunction against the distribution of a particular book, the suit is one in equity, and there is no trial by jury. Trial is by a judge, and the judge thereby becomes the censor. If he finds the book to be "obscene," no bookseller will distribute it. For distribution would mean criminal prosecution. Section 22-a of New York City's Code of Criminal Procedure likewise provides for action for a permanent injunction to prohibit the sale of obscene material. This provision has been held constitutional by the United States Supreme Court.

While the courts will seldom upset a finding of fact that a particular publication is "obscene," they will take a long look at the constitutionality of the state statute or municipal ordinance under which a prosecution is brought. In essence, any statute which seeks to go beyond the traditional concepts of lewdness and obscenity to strike down, for example, the "sacrilegious," or "accounts of crime, lust and bloodshed," are held to be too vague to be constitutional. In like manner, a Maryland statute prohibiting the display of "crime and lust" magazines to minors has been declared invalid; a state court ruled that the prohibition can lie only against sale.

Motion Pictures

In 1915, the Supreme Court, holding that movies were strictly entertainment and not within the orbit of constitutional protection, upheld the constitutionality of movie censorship. For nearly four decades, this decision stood unchallenged. But in 1952, in a case involving the highly controversial motion picture, *The Miracle*, the Court decided that refusal to license the picture on the grounds that it was "sacrilegious," was a violation of the Constitution. Shortly thereafter, the Court likewise reversed bans on films that had been condemned for "immorality," "inciting to crime and violence," and "inciting to racial tension." In all these cases, the Court ruled that the standards set by the statutes were too vague to be constitutional, and indiciated that only a ban on the basis of "obscenity" under a narrowly drawn statute could be sustained.

The effect of the Supreme Court actions has been to bring motion pictures within the protection of the First

Amendment. As a result, movie censorship machinery has begun to fall apart. Whereas, in 1950, seven states maintained state censorship machinery, by 1957, only New York State could claim a formidable state censorship system, and it is clear that the burden of proof of "obscenity" has now been shifted to the censor. Some 58 municipalities still maintain municipal censorship, but significantly, one of the most vigorous and controversial censorship boards, that in Memphis, Tenn., was ended by a 41-4 vote of a special Mayor's Committee.

Elsewhere, the Oregon Supreme Court invalidated the application of the state's anti-obscenity law to motion pictures, and the Georgia Supreme Court ruled that an Atlanta ordinance requiring permits for the exhibition of the movies was a violation of the state constitution. Atlanta therefore passed a new ordinance providing for the reviewing of all films and their classification as "approved," "unsuitable for the young," or "objectionable." A Superior Court judge struck down the ordinance, ruling that Atlanta had no authority to enact it. In Maryland, the legislature defeated an effort to require the labelling of certain films "For Adults Only." Yet, in 1961, the Supreme Court, in what appeared to be a reversal of the trend it had started, upheld the constitutionality of state and municipal boards of censorship, and in a 5-4 decision, upheld the right of the Chicago police to pre-screen the Austrian film, *Don Juan*.

Censorship on the Federal Level

Censorship on the federal level operates in three major areas: (1) radio and TV; (2) the mails; (3) import of foreign reading matter.

RADIO AND TV: The Federal Communications Commission licenses the operation of radio and TV stations. Since there are many more applicants than there are frequencies, in granting or renewing a license, the FCC must make a choice between competing applicants.

In setting minimum standards for a station licensee, the FCC, in addition to its technical and operational requirements, prescribes a basic program code that may be summarized as follows.

a. Monopoly is discouraged. While a newspaper may be granted a license to operate a radio station, it will not be granted a license where the combined radio and newspaper control would give a communication monopoly in a community.

b. Nothing obscene or indecent may be uttered over the airwaves. While the FCC has no power to censor a broadcast nor even to issue a cease and desist order, it can suspend or subsequently deny the reissue of a license.

c. On controversial issues, where a station has given radio time to one point of view, it must provide, when requested to do so, an equal amount of time to the opposing point of view. In general, the FCC favors free time to both sides in the presentation of a controversial issue.

d. A station owner may not use his station to express his own views on controversial issues. The FCC has rejected the argument that a station owner should have the same right to express his views as a newspaper publisher. The FCC points out that while newspapers are private enterprises, radio stations are licensed by the public.

e. In the granting or renewal of a license, the FCC will take into consideration the record of an applicant or station operator with respect to his fairness of approach to the various ethnic and social groups within the community. Stations sponsoring or allotting program time to "hate" groups or deliberately excluding a pro-labor point of view from the air run the risk of losing their licenses, when they come up for renewal.

MAILS: By federal law and by post office regulations, obscene or fraudulent matter is barred from the mails, as is the use of the mails to conduct a lottery or to engage in other specified unlawful activity. In addition, matter which violates the provisions of the Federal Espionage Act is also barred.

Where the mails are being used to carry obscene publications or as a means of fraudulent representation, the Post Office may either exclude such publications totally from the mails, or where the publisher or distributor enjoys a second class mailing privilege, may revoke this privilege. In the past, where matter has been banned from the mails, there has usually been no hearing; where revocation of second class mailing privilege is involved, there has generally been a hearing before the postal authorities.

Since the attempt to mail forbidden matter is a criminal offense, post office action, at one and the same time, may ban a particular item from the mails, and by so doing, render the party that sought to mail the item criminally liable. Here, censorship does not prevent the risk of criminal prosecution, but creates it.

Up until quite recently, there was only a very narrow court review of the actions of the postal authorities. In the *Esquire* case, however, substantial inroads were made on Post Office censorship. The Post Office had sought to deny the second class mailing privileges of Esquire Magazine, chiefly on the grounds that it did not contain information of a public character.

The case was taken up to the Supreme Court which decided that the authority of the Post Office nowhere includes the right to revoke mailing privileges because a publication does not contain information of a public character. The revocation of Esquire mailing privileges was reversed, the Court holding that the Post Office may no longer deny second class mailing privileges because of the contents of a publication. It may, however, after hearing, declare particular issues of publications, books or pamphlets nonmailable.

At about the same time that the *Esquire* case was in the courts, orders barring from the mails a publication on birth control and another on sex adjustment in marriage were reversed by federal courts. Since the *Esquire* decision, the Post Office has been very cautious in the exercise of its powers to ban on grounds of obscenity. In fact, several Supreme Court justices have doubted the P.O.'s power to ban as distinguished from bringing criminal proceedings. However, mail fraud orders continue to be issued wherever the postal authorities feel that matter being mailed contains exaggerated claims. (The subject of false advertising is beyond the scope of this work.)

IMPORT OF FOREIGN READING MATTER: The Customs Bureau exercises preliminary power in screening foreign produced reading matter and films for obscenity or for advocating or urging treason, insurrection or forcible resistance to any law of the United States. However, customs inspectors do not have the final decision. Court proceedings are required to confiscate or destroy a book for obscenity or other stated reasons. Either party can demand a jury trial.

Fair Comment v. Contempt

Since the famed trial of Peter Zenger, the New York printer, for sedition in colonial times, the freedom of newspapers from restriction has been synonymous with freedom of the press. As a result, attempted censorship of newspapers has never been extensive. The major issue has revolved around devices for preventing hostile newspaper criticism of public officials.

A Minnesota law of 1925, known as the "Minnesota Gag Law," provided for injunction against malicious, scandalous, defamatory and obscene newspapers, magazines and publications. Truth was a defense only if matter was published with good motives and for justifiable ends. Injunction could be granted not only against objectionable issues of newspapers or publications but could completely stop a newspaper or publication from publishing. The Supreme Court invalidated this statute as an improper interference with freedom of the press.

The Supreme Court likewise struck down a more subtle attempt at press censorship by Huey Long in Louisiana. He sought to impose a 2% tax on the gross receipts of newspapers selling ad space and having a circulation of more than 20,000 per week. The law was aimed at the larger newspapers which were opposed to the Long administration. The Court held the law to be a violation of freedom of press as well as unlawful discrimination against the larger newspapers in Louisiana.

Contempt proceedings have been the most effective device for dealing with criticism of public officials, particularly judges. A newspaper editor or publisher, fearful lest criticism of official action might lead to criminal prosecution, tends to be extremely cautious in his handling of news and issues involving court cases.

In recent years, the Supreme Court has completely liberalized the law applicable to contempt proceedings. Unless the criticism creates a "clear and present danger" to the fair and orderly administration of justice, it cannot be punished summarily for contempt. The Supreme Court, in urging judges to be less sensitive to criticism, estimates that judges have too much stamina to yield to unseemly pressures.

Under the rules governing contempt, critical comment after a proceeding is concluded can never be punished, because there is no interference with the proceedings which can result from the criticism. As to comment made while proceedings are in progress, only comment specifically intended to influence and capable of influencing the jury, or implying a threat to the judge or jurymen, or inciting public opinion against the judge or jury with specific intent to influence their judgments may be punished.

In recent years, contempt proceedings have been used as a weapon in the desegregation struggle. The Supreme Court has now thrown out a $500,000 libel judgment awarded a Montgomery, Ala. city official in a suit against the New York Times and four Negro ministers. The Court ruled that a public official may not recover damages for a defamatory falsehood relating to his official conduct without a showing of actual malice, of knowledge the statement was false or reckless disregard of whether or not it was false. Justices Black, Douglas and Goldberg, in concurring opinions, enunciated a doctrine of unconditional freedom of the public and press to criticize official conduct.

B. Police Power Regulation

As has been previously noted, freedom of expression does not cover the obscene, the fraudulent or the libelous. Such expression is regarded as not being part of the exposition of an idea, and therefore not "speech" at all, in the sense that the First Amendment to the Constitution seeks to protect.

But there is speech that is part of the exposition of an idea which may, nevertheless, be subject to regulation. What, for example, is the law when a belief is expressed that is offensive to other persons? Or, when the method of expression fails to meet certain basic requirements?

In general, the answers to these questions involve a weighing of the freedom of expression, on the one hand, against the regulatory police power of the state, on the other. Through the 1940's, the Supreme Court, in a series of cases dealing with the efforts of the respective states to curb the Jehovah's Witnesses, a religious sect often displaying substantial fanaticism, came close to giving full rein to freedom of expression. The freedoms guaranteed by the First Amendment were said to be "preferred liberties." More recently, this full freedom has been somewhat circumscribed by the Court, and the right of the state to regulate in behalf of the welfare of its people has come to be entitled to equal consideration. The rules, as they emerge from a welter of somewhat confusing opinions, may be summarized as follows:

Prior Restraints; Licensing

If Mr. X expresses his religious views on a street corner, he cannot be prevented from doing so either by the police or by municipal ordinance. This is equally true for the streets of a privately owned company town. If he were to distribute handbills on the streets, or ring doorbells soliciting funds for his religious cause, he could not be forbidden to do so. Moreover, he cannot be required to seek a permit to distribute handbills. Nor can he be made to pay a license fee or tax to sell pamphlets of a religious nature on the streets or by door-to-door canvass. If, however, he is a commercial magazine peddler, his door-to-door canvassing can be regulated.

Mr. X can be required to register with the police for

11

purposes of identification if he desires to solicit funds. This is regarded as a means of protecting the community against possible fraud. But he cannot be required to salute the flag as a condition of his distributing literature or soliciting funds.

If Mr. X desires to organize a religious parade through the streets of his city, he can be required to obtain a license, so long as the licensing official has no discretion to censor the purpose of the parade, but only the authority to weigh considerations of traffic, public safety, etc. In like manner an open-air park meeting can be licensed, but not on the basis of content of the speeches. The obstruction of public passageways and thoroughfares can be forbidden by law enforcement authorities, and likewise, the authorities can determine the appropriate uses for parks and recreational facilities. What is forbidden the licensing authority is the right to discriminate between one cause and another in terms of granting a license.

Punishment of Breach of the Peace or Disorderly Conduct

If, in the course of a private discussion, Mr. X makes offensive references to religions other than his own, there is no question of his right to express his opinions. But if he were to come uninvited into a hotel or privately owned establishment, insisting on making his opinions known to unwilling listeners, he could be convicted of disorderly conduct. Freedom of expression does not include the right to interfere with another's enjoyment of his property.

But if he makes the same remarks at a public meeting place, he can be successfully prosecuted only if his remarks incite to riot or to a breach of the peace. Moreover, he is legally accountable only for a breach of the peace that results from his own incitation, but not for a breach of the peace that is occasioned by the reactions of his antagonists.

The mere possibility of disturbance is not enough; to warrant prosecution, the breach must be imminent or actual. In the absence of such clearcut breach of the peace, prosecution and conviction are possible only under a statute narrowly drawn to define and punish specific conduct as constituting a *clear and present danger* to a substantial interest of the state. Some states, particularly sensitive to attacks against racial, religious and ethnic groups, have adopted such specific, narrowly drawn statutes. "Race Hate" laws seek to punish the incitement to or advocacy of hatred against particular ethnic or religious groups in the community. "Group Libel" laws empower the Attorney-General of a state to prosecute those who, with malicious intent to promote hatred, issue false written or printed material about particular ethnic, racial or religious groups in the community. State laws of one or the other type described exist in Illinois, Indiana, Massachusetts, New Mexico and New Jersey, but they are seldom invoked. The New Jersey law was declared unconstitutional in 1942 for being too vague and indefinite.

The First Amendment, however, does not protect profane or abusive language. If Mr. X, on being accosted by a police officer, uses abusive and profane language, he can be prosecuted for disorderly conduct. In like manner, the First Amendment protects normal speech, but may not protect speech that is amplified by a loud-speaker or sound-truck apparatus. The Supreme Court has made clear that regulations as to time, place and volume of sound are constitutional, and has even intimated that, although a municipality may not license sound trucks, they may be banned altogether.

If Mr. X in expressing his religious opinions, advocates the doing of something that is against the law, he may be prosecuted and convicted. But the law under which he is prosecuted must be specific and definite. The Supreme Court reversed the conviction of a group of Mormons who had advocated polygamy in one of their publications, and the case was remanded to Utah courts to consider whether the law under which they had been prosecuted was "vague and indefinite."

Where a valid licensing procedure exists, Mr. X cannot take the law into his own hands by arranging for a parade without a license after he had been denied a license. The Supreme Court has held that the aggrieved party must seek court assistance in ordering the issuance of a license, but cannot proceed without a license.

Peddlers of Ideas

What emerges from the foregoing is that the "peddler of ideas" is generally free from prior restraint that smacks of censorship of his views. Taxes, discretionary licensing arrangements and discriminatory administrative regulations are invalid. However, considerations of public welfare, use of public property, traffic control and similar factors, consistently applied, can furnish the basis for a valid licensing system. In general, speech itself is freer than the availability of public places for it. Convictions for breach of the peace or disorderly conduct will be sustained only if it can be affirmatively shown that an actual or imminent breach of the peace occurred and that it was directly caused by the advocacy of the defendant.

II. PROTECTION OF NATIONAL SECURITY

Thus far, we have dealt essentially with the problems created when the individual's rights under the First Amendment are pitted against the general welfare of a local community. In this area, the courts have not hesitated to provide maximum play for freedom of expression. Much more troublesome is the task of determining how far a free and democratic society is obliged to extend its freedom to individuals or organizations dedicated to the overthrow of its form of government. In weighing individual freedom against the requirements of national security, courts and legislatures alike have been faced with the most penetrating problem of our times.

The government has never been powerless to deal with *crimes of action* against the state. There have always been adequate laws on the books against treason, sabotage, espionage and various activities designed to weaken our military or industrial establishments. These laws generally do not involve a conflict between individual freedom and national security.

It is at the point that the government seeks to define and

14

punish *crimes of advocacy* that the issue of freedom of expression of the individual is drawn. As to when advocacy may be punished, the tests laid down by the Supreme Court have differed from period to period, generally depending on the state of the nation and the shape of world affairs at a given time.

In the aftermath of World War I, for example, when the government rode herd on anarchists, syndicalists and a variety of political radicals, advocacy of a point of view could be punished if it exhibited a *"dangerous tendency."* The vast network of state laws outlawing red flags, and seeking to punish anarchists, syndicalists and the exponents of similar political ideas were generally sustained on the grounds that such advocacy created a *dangerous tendency* in the direction of bringing about what was being advocated by the spokesman. It made no difference under this test whether what was being advocated could in fact be feasibly brought about.

During the thirties, the Court took another look at political radicalism, and found it to be much less of a threat to the national security. Accordingly, what had been the minority point of view as expounded by such jurists as Holmes and Brandeis, emerged as the majority opinion, and the Court held that for advocacy to be punished, it had to create a *"clear and present danger"* of bringing about the very evil with which the state had the right to deal. Just as the *dangerous tendency* test almost inevitably led to sustaining conviction, the *clear and present danger* test almost inevitably led to reversing conviction. Under this test, for example, a Communist preaching the overthrow of the government, could not be punished for his utterances unless there was a *clear and present danger* demonstrated that his utterances would lead to action.

During the forties, a reaction began to set in against the "pure" doctrine of the *clear and present danger* test. The feeling grew, as expressed in a variety of federal legislation, that mature political philosophies such as fascism and communism posed a threat to the national security of this country, so severe that it was not feasible to await a clear

15

and present danger before advocacy could be restrained. The Court grappled with this problem through a number of situations, finally emerging in the *Dennis* case (the trial of the eleven top Communists under the Smith Act) with a new test—*clear and probable danger*—a sort of middle ground between *dangerous tendency* and *clear and present danger*. Although the language used by the Court is the *Dennis* case is actually the language of the *clear and present danger test*, the meaning of the decision is that the government has the right to restrain advocacy when what is advocated creates an indicated likelihood that some action will be taken to bring it about. Students of civil liberties have treated this decision as establishing a test of *clear and probable danger*.

Against this background, it is possible to study the security machinery of the federal and state governments and the impact of this machinery on the status of civil liberty.

A. Sedition and Subversion

The first piece of sedition legislation was the Alien and Sedition Acts of 1798, which authorized the President to deport aliens whom he judged to be dangerous to the peace and safety of the country, and sought to punish false and scandalous writings against the government or any of its arms, if published with intent to defame or to excite hatred. These measures were enacted at a time when the country was not actually at war. History records that they aroused powerful popular indignation which all but destroyed the Federalist Party. With the advent of Thomas Jefferson to the presidency, those imprisoned under the Sedition Law were pardoned and all fines collected were eventually repaid.

In our time, the first important sedition act was the Espionage Act of 1917, passed after our entry into the First World War. During the twenties, the pattern of prosecution for sedition in wartime was carried over to peacetime through the anarchy, syndicalism and sedition laws of the states, mentioned above. Then, in 1940, a federal peacetime sedition law was passed for the first time since 1798. This was contained in the Alien Registration Act of 1940, sometimes called the Smith Act. Analysis of both the Espionage Act of 1917 and the Smith Act will help the reader to understand the security machinery and the civil liberties considerations as well.

War Measures

The Espionage Act of 1917, which is still on the books and applied in the Second World War as well as the First, defines three wartime offenses: (1) the willful utterance of false statement with intent to interfere with the operation or success of the armed forces of the United States; (2) the willful causing of or attempt to cause insubordination, disloyalty, mutiny or refusal of duty in the armed forces of the United States: (3) the willful obstruction of the recruiting or enlistment service of the United States. Penalties of fine of not more than $10,000 or imprisonment for not more than twenty years or both are provided. (An Amendment to this Act, passed in 1918, added nine additional offenses. The Amendment was repealed in 1921.)

The enforcement of these provisions of the Espionage Act differed widely in the two world wars. In the First World War, there were hundreds of prosecutions of persons who raised their voices against the draft and against the war. Many publications were banned from the mails and their second class mailing privileges revoked for similar utterances. In general, the courts took the position that an utterance did not have to create a "clear and present danger" to the war effort; it was sufficient if the utterance created a "dangerous tendency." Moreover, willful intent was presumed from the speech or writing. Under these tests, conviction followed almost inevitably on prosecution.

In the Second World War, there were relatively few prosecutions under the Espionage Act. Generally, they were limited to prosecutions of members of certain Negro sects for conspiring to obstruct the operation of selective service, to members of the German-American Bund and to organizations and members of organizations professionally anti-Semitic, anti-government and pro-Axis.

17

The government and the courts took action only where there was actual incitement to violation of the law or where there was a "clear and present danger" that the illegal action urged would be taken. The Supreme Court, in the two Espionage cases which it reviewed, reversed convictions—in one case, of 28 German-American Bund leaders who had advised their members to resist certain provisions of the 1940 Draft Act which were alleged to discriminate against Bund members—in the second case, of a Chicago pamphleteer who had prepared and distributed mimeographed circulars which discouraged recruiting and enlistment. This latter case most certainly would have been decided the other way in World War I, indicating that the government gave much greater latitude to freedom of expression in the Second World War than in the First.

The Federal Peacetime Sedition Act

The Alien Registration Act of 1940 (Smith Act), to a greater extent than the Espionage Act, posed the major issues involving sedition in the Second World War. As observed previously, this law was the first peacetime Sedition Law to be enacted by Congress since 1798.

Section 1 of the Act makes the Espionage Act applicable in peacetime. Section 2 enumerates the following offenses: (1) willfully advocating the overthrow of government in the United States by force or violence; (2) willfully issuing any written or printed matter so advocating; (3) to organize any society, group or assembly of persons who so advocate; (4) to become a member of or affiliate with any such society, group or assembly, knowing its purposes. Section 3 makes it unlawful to attempt or conspire to commit the prohibited acts. The penalty is fine up to $10,000, imprisonment up to 10 years, or both.

The most significant wartime case involving the Sedition Act was the prosecution for seditious conspiracy brought in the federal court of the District of Columbia against some 29 leaders of alleged pro-Nazi movements. (This is not the Bund prosecution, mentioned above.) The action was begun in 1942 under both the Sedition Act and the

Espionage Act. The court threw out the "Sedition" indictment on the grounds that the Sedition Act could not punish conduct prior to 1940. The "Espionage" charges were dropped because the government was unable to uncover evidence of illegal activities after this country had gone to war.

In 1944, new indictments were brought, charging conspiracy on behalf of the German government to undermine the morale of the armed forces. Upon the death of the presiding judge in 1945, prosecution was not resumed and the proceeding lapsed.

A case only slightly less celebrated was the prosecution of the Socialist Workers Party (Trotskyites) and the CIO Teamsters' Union in Minneapolis on the charge that they advocated the overthrow of the government by force and violence. The prosecution rested its case on writings advocating the overthrow of the government contained in Party publications. A Workers Defense Guard, created to protect union property against destruction, was charged with being the organized means through which the attempt to overthrow the government was to be made. Although this second charge was subsequently dismissed, convictions of 18 of the persons prosecuted were secured.

Notwithstanding the fact that the case posed the issue of the constitutionality of the first federal peacetime sedition act since 1798, the Supreme Court refused to review the conventions. The lower courts rejected the argument that the prosecution should be dismissed because there was no "clear and present danger" of overthrow of the government by this group. They held that the federal statute, by specifically making it a crime to advocate overthrow of the government by force and violence, has rendered the existence of a "clear and present danger" immaterial.

The case of *Dennis* v. *United States* (341 U. S. 494, 1951) provided an answer to the constitutionality of the Smith Act. The case involved the legality of the convictions of eleven top Communists for conspiracy to advocate the overthrow of the government under the Smith Act. It should be noted that the crime charged was *conspiracy* and that the element of the crime was not the overthrow of the government or even action in that direction, but only *advocacy* of such overthrow. In upholding the convictions, the Supreme Court upheld the constitutionality of the Smith Act, took judicial note of the menace of Communist subversive machinery and, as noted above, (see p. 16) revised the test as to when advocacy may be punished:

"In each case (courts) must ask whether the gravity of the evil, discounted by its improbability, justifies such invasion of free speech as is necessary to avoid the danger."

In 1957, the Court subtly modified its decision in the *Dennis* case. In a case involving the conviction of a group of California Communist Party leaders, a distinction was drawn between "'advocacy of forcible overthrow as mere abstract doctrine" and "advocacy which incites to illegal action." In reversing the convictions, the Court held that the judge's charge to the jury in the lower court had been erroneous. Five of the defendants were freed and nine others were ordered retried.

Yet, in the *Scales* case (1961), the Court upheld the constitutionality of the membership clause of the Smith Act making it a crime knowingly to belong to a party that advocates the forcible overthrow of the government.

State Sedition Laws

Prior to World War I, most of the states of the union contented themselves with statutes specifying the common law offenses of "riot," "unlawful assembly," "breach of the peace," and "disorderly conduct." The common denominator of each of these offenses is conduct of an individual or group which threatens an immediate disturbance of the public peace or an immediate violation of the rights of others. In other words, conduct which creates a *clear and present danger* of an evil which the state has the power to regulate.

With the coming of World War I, however, the states turned increasingly to law which would punish utterances as well as acts. During the First World War, many of the states supplemented federal legislation with espionage acts of their own, often substantially more stringent. A Minnesota statute for example made it unlawful to say that men should not enlist in the armed forces of the United States or that residents of Minnesota should not aid in carrying on war with our enemies.

Similar laws were passed in Florida, Iowa, Louisiana, Missouri, Montana, Nebraska, New Hampshire, New Jersey, Pennsylvania, Texas, West Virginia and Wisconsin.

In the aftermath of World War I, the increasing hostility to Radicals reinforced this mood and led to the passage of a rash of state sedition laws, designed to limit the freedom of expression of these groups in peacetime. The statutes include: (1) red flag laws; (2) criminal anarchy, syndicalism and sedition laws; (3) laws directed against Communists and the Communist Party.

In a previous edition of this volume, substantial attention was given to an analysis of each of these types of state laws which, in one form or another, exist in every state of the union. But in April, 1956, the Supreme Court in a 6-3 decision in *Pennsylvania* v. *Nelson* held that Federal legislation has pre-empted the area of prosecution for sedition. The highest court made clear that the *Nelson* case concerned only sedition against the United States, and that the dominant interest of the federal government precludes state intervention, and that administration of state acts would conflict with federal operations.

The reaction to the Supreme Court decision on the part of the attorneys-general of the states was strongly critical, and legislation was introduced in Congress to revalidate the state sedition laws. The legislation, however, never reached the floor of either house. More recently, the states have sought to give new meaning to ther sedition laws by instituting suits alleging sedition against the *state*, as distinguished from the *nation*. It seems clear, however, that this legislation has been rendered archaic and largely ineffective by the Court's action.

And yet, it may be helpful to summarize what can and cannot be done under state sedition laws:

. . . It is clearly constitutional to punish the open and direct advocacy of assassination, sabotage, destruction of property and other violent and unlawful conduct.

. . . It is probably not constitutional to convict a person under a sedition law for nothing more than membership in an organization which, as part of its program, advocates violent action. There should be some evidence of affirmative personal support for violent action to warrant conviction.

. . . It is probably not constitutional to convict a person under a sedition law for possessing and distributing literature of an organization which as part of its program advocates violent action, where the literature involved does not itself advocate either violence or unlawful acts.

. . . It is probably not constitutional to convict for peaceable advocacy of remote objectives, presently illegal.

Disclosure Requirements for Subversives

Several pieces of federal legislation are aimed at compelling disclosure of subversive agents and activities. The Foreign Agents' Registration Act of 1938, amended in 1953, requires the agents of any "foreign principal" to register with the Department of Justice, to file statements about their activities and affairs, and to identify any "political propaganda" they circulate.

The Alien Registration Act of 1940 (Smith Act), supplemented by the Immigration and Nationality Act of 1952 (see below p. 23), requires all resident aliens in this country to be "registered" and fingerprinted and requires comprehensive information about them.

The Internal Security Act of 1950 requires the registration of "Communist action" or 'Communist-front" organizations. The procedures set out for achieving such registration are quite complex, and no organization has registered up to this point. Under the Communist Control Act of 1954, "Communist-infiltrated" organizations were added to the two groups required to register under the 1950 Act.

The Supreme Court in 1961 ruled the Internal Security Act Constitutional.

On the state level, disclosure requirements have become a weapon in the desegregation struggle. In an effort to deter Negro activity, several southern states have sought to ban the National Association for the Advancement of Colored People and to require disclosure of its membership lists. The Supreme Court ruled in 1958, in setting aside a $100,000 fine for contempt levied against the NAACP by the State of Alabama, that compulsory disclosure of membership lists is unconstitutional. In *Bates* v. *Little Rock* (1960), the Supreme Court upheld a lower court ruling voiding Arkansas laws which compel organizations to disclose membership and finances, and permit examination of records without warrant.

Alien Subversion

The policy of excluding aliens believed to be subversive dates from 1903, when we began barring anarchists. Deportation of undesirable aliens, however, goes back as far as 1798 and the Alien and Sedition Acts. Under the Internal Security Act of 1950, Communists and other totalitarians were specifically denied entry to this country, and under the Immigration and Nationality Act of 1952 (Walter-McCarran Act), the provisions were made even more stringent. Under this Act, an alien may be barred from entry if any consular official or the Attorney-General knows or has reasonable grounds to believe that he will engage in activities contrary to the public security.

The 1952 Act also bars from naturalization Communists, members of Communist or Communist-front organizations, and all persons who teach, advocate or publish the violent overthrow of the government. The ban is retroactive on those who within ten years of the application for naturalization have belonged in one of these classes. In addition, the 1952 Act sets out new grounds for denaturalization—concealing at the time of naturalization that one was a member of a subversive organization; refusing, within ten years following naturalization, to testify before a congressional committee with regard to subversive activities if the person has been convicted of contempt because of such refusal; becoming, within five years after naturalization, a member of an organization where such membership in the first place would have prevented naturalization.

Finally, the 1952 Act adds a provision permitting the deportation of any alien who is, or who at any time after his entry into the country has been a member of the various organizations designated as subversive. This makes mandatory the deportation of an alien who at any time after his entry was a Communist even though he may long since have left the Party, and has even required deportation where an alien joined an organization without really understanding its purposes. The statute allows the Attorney General in certain limited cases to suspend deportation, and private bills have occasionally been introduced in Congress to prevent deportation under particularly tragic personal circumstances.

The effect of recent provisions affecting immigration, naturalization, denaturalization and deportation have tended to leave little room for Court action. This is uniquely a field for congressional legislation, and with the tightening of requirements under the Walter-McCarran Act, the courts have been powerless even in situations where the accused appear to be innocent victims. Thus, it is possible to deport a man today for views or associations which he held twenty-five years ago. This creates a double standard of citizenship as between the American-born and the naturalized citizen. While the American-born citizen cannot be convicted for sedition on the basis of "guilt by association," the concept of "guilt by association" is made expressly applicable by the immigration and naturalization laws to naturalized citizens.

B. Loyalty and Security

Religious Liberty and Loyalty

In general, the majority of Protestant sects, the Catholic Church and the Jewish faith render "unto Caesar the things that are Caesar's." Obligations of citizenship, such

24

as saluting the flag or the bearing of arms in defense of the nation, are not considered to be inconsistent with religious conviction.

Certain religious sects, however, such as the Jehovah's Witnesses, forbid the salute to the flag on the grounds that it is idolatry. The Witnesses, Quakers and Seventh Day Adventists forbid the bearing of arms in defense of one's country. Persons adhering to the doctrines of these religious sects are faced with a sharp conflict between their religious conscience and the obligations of citizenship. In addition, many pacifists, as a matter of conscience, will not go to war. Where religious belief or conscience clashes with obligations of citizenship, a legal issue is created.

SALUTING THE FLAG: Most of the states have some laws designed to teach respect for the flag. There are requirements that the flag be displayed over or within public school buildings. Some states require flag programs and special instruction concerning the flag in the public schools. In approximately 12 states, there are varying provisions requiring that students salute the flag. These states are Arizona, Delaware, Idaho, Kansas, Maryland, Massachussets, Nebraska, New Jersey, New York, Rhode Island and Washington.

The question has arisen under these laws whether a person whose religious scruples forbid saluting the flag can refuse to do so. Prior to 1943, state courts in Georgia, Massachusetts, New York and Pennsylvania, as well as the Supreme Court, held that religious conviction was not sufficient reason to justify refusal to salute the flag.

In 1943, however, the Supreme Court reversed its decision, to hold that a child cannot be expelled from the public schools for refusing to salute the flag. The Court pointed out that a refusal to salute the flag that is based on religious conviction does not indicate disrespect for the flag. To compel a person to salute the flag against his religious scruples is an unreasonable exercise of state power.

CONSCIENTIOUS OBJECTION TO MILITARY SERVICE: Where freedom of religion conflicts with national safety and security, the courts have held that the constitutional protection must give way. Thus, while one may safely refuse to salute the flag for reasons of religious conviction, it is only by the grace of Congress that the duty to bear arms in defense of the nation may be altered or avoided.

To an increasing extent, the Congress of the United States has given official recognition, through the last two wars, to the religious beliefs, or convictions of conscience of persons refusing to bear arms in defense of the nation. Under the 1941 Selective Training and Service Act, persons conscientiously opposed to participation in war, if their objection were sustained by the local draft board, could be assigned to non-combatant service. Those opposed even to noncombatant service could be assigned to work of "national importance under civilian direction." In general, persons refusing both combatant and noncombatant service were assigned to civilian "C.O." work camps, which were administered with military discipline. Failure to report for induction either into the Armed Forces or into a "C.O." camp was a basis for prosecution, conviction and imprisonment.

Under the 1948 draft legislation, assignment to "C.O." camp was eliminated. A person sustaining the fact that religious conviction bars him from military service is entitled to deferment. However, the legislation requires a belief in a Supreme Being to entitle a person to qualify for such deferment. Thus, atheistic pacifists are not protected. The legislative history reveals that this provision was included to prevent Communists from shirking military duty. Under the 1951 Selective Service Act, the law was changed to require two years of civilian work in an approved government or non-profit agency. In general, it is only the "absolutist," who refuses to cooperate in any way, and the atheist conscientious objector who faces punishment for his refusal to serve.

Another issue in connection with "conscientious objectors" has been the admission to citizenship of aliens, otherwise satisfactory, who declare their refusal to bear arms in defense of the Constitution. In 1929 and again in

1931, the Supreme Court reversed the granting of citizenship to persons who, because of pacifist or religious beliefs, stated that they could not take an oath "to defend the Constitution and laws of the United States against all enemies" where such defense required the bearing of arms. The Court stated that the right of an alien to become a citizen is not a natural, but a law-given right, and that citizenship must be denied to those who do not measure up strictly to the requirements for naturalization.

In 1946, the Supreme Court reversed these earlier decisions, holding that the oath to defend the Constitution does not specifically require the bearing of arms. Basic to the decision, however, is the premise that Congress could require an oath to bear arms, if it wanted to do so. In that event, the Constition would not protect the refusal to take such an oath.

Political Disloyalty

While the issue involved in clashes between religious belief and responsibilities of citizenship is more accurately characterized as one of non-comformity, the question of association with organizations and views that are subversive of the American form of government clearly poses the clash between freedom of expression and loyalty. This has emerged as perhaps the major problem in the delicate balancing of individual freedom and national security. For, notwithstanding the existence of legislation, both federal and state, to deal with sedition, the major methods for dealing with subversive activities in the post-World War II period have been (1) the loyalty-security programs promulgated by the executive branch of the government, and (2) legislative investigations into loyalty and subversion.

LOYALTY-SECURITY PROGRAMS: The background of investigations into loyalty of government employees dates from 1939 when Congress passed the Hatch Act, among other things, making it unlawful for any government employee to have "membership in any political party or organization which advocates the overthrow of our constitutional form of government in the United States." This was followed in 1941 by a Congressional appropriation to the FBI to inquire into subversive activities among government employees and by the attachment of riders to appropriations bills forbidding payment to persons who advocated or were members of organizations advocating the overthrow of the government of the United States. As applied to cut off the salaries of several federal employees during the war, these riders were declared unconstitional as bills of attainder. (A bill of attainder is one by which a legislature finds a person guilty of an offense and seeks to punish him for it without court trial.)

During the war, a start toward a comprehensive loyalty check for executive employees was undertaken. This reached a climax in 1946 when President Truman promulgated his Loyalty Order requiring investigation of all employees in the executive branch and of all persons seeking employment.

On its first promulgation, the program called for denying federal employment when "on all the evidence, reasonable grounds exist for the belief that the person involved is disloyal to the government of the United States." In 1951 the President altered the Order to bar persons about whose loyalty there was "reasonable doubt." In order to establish criteria by which disloyalty could be measured, the Order required the compiling by the Attorney General of a list of subversive organizations. Originally, this list was developed without any hearings and without any opportunity on the part of listed organizations to dispute the claim of being subversive. In 1951, however, the Supreme Court decided that for the Attorney General to place organizations on a subversive list without giving them a hearing was not permissible.

In 1953, President Eisenhower revised the "Loyalty" program of the Truman Administration. The Eisenhower "Security" program was designed to eliminate government employees who were security risks, although not necessarily disloyal. And, by seeking to reenforce the distinction between *disloyalty* and *security risk,* the program sought to take some of the onus off being fired from a federal job.

The Eisenhower program set up as the basic test of employee fitness a finding that "retention in employment in the federal service of the person being investigated is clearly consistent with the interests of national security." In the administration of this program, departmental loyalty boards and security officers are not limited to the use of the Attorney General's list. In 1956, the Supreme Court placed limitations on the administration of the Security program by ruling, in a 6-3 decision, that federal employees can be dismissed as security risks only if they hold sensitive jobs. The Court further held that President Eisenhower erred in 1953, when by executive order, he had extended security regulations to cover *all* government workers.

For the most part, the states do not have elaborate loyalty-security programs for the screening of state employees. Public school teachers constitute a notable exception, although even here permanent machinery does not exist in most states. New York State has a Security Risk Law, which authorizes the Civil Service Commission to screen all applicants for state jobs.

On the whole, however, the states use other techniques. In some, members of the Communist Party are kept off the election ballot by law. These include Arkansas, California, Delaware, Illinois, Indiana, Ohio, Pennsylvania, Tennessee and Wisconsin. In others, public officers and employees are screened by requiring them to take a loyalty oath. The Ober Law in Maryland and the Broyles Law in Illinois are typical. (See below, p. 30, for a discussion of loyalty oaths.)

In addition to federal and state loyalty programs, since part of the government's defense work is done under contract by private industry, security screening is required by executive order of those employed by private industry in carrying on classified projects or contracts. In addition, security programs have been developed by some private industries on their own initiative, even though they may not be engaged in defense work. As to organized labor, in addition to loyalty oath provisions in the Taft-Hartley Act, the Communist Control Act of 1954 has provisions for identifying "Communist-infiltrated organizations," and if a labor union is found to be infiltrated it forfeits its privileges of collective bargaining.

LOYALTY OATHS: In general, the Federal government has not found it necessary to impose loyalty oaths on government personnel, probably because the loyalty-security program has been regarded as adequate. The Taft-Hartley Act, however, imposes a loyalty oath requirement on the officers of labor unions, a provision which the Supreme Court has held to be constitutional.

The Gwinn Amendment (1952) bars from federal housing units any person who is a member of any organization designated as subversive by the Attorney General. In the enforcement of the Amendment—actually, a rider to federal housing legislation—local housing authorities have required oaths of prospective tenants. Such requirements have been declared unconstitutional by state courts in California, Illinois, New Jersey and Wisconsin. It is doubtful whether the Gwinn Amendment is still law, since the legislation to which it was appended has been superseded. However, several local housing authorities continue to require loyalty oaths of tenants.

It is principally among the states, however, that a pervasive loyalty oath requirement has developed. In general, it takes the form of a sworn disavowal of present and past membership in the Communist Party or in designated organizations. A five year period of past loyalty is the usual standard. The concept of many of these oaths is that membership in an organization on the Attorney General's list is conclusive of unfitness for public employment. This goes beyond the President's loyalty-security order and is counter to federal court pronouncements that membership in designated organizations cannot be regarded as conclusive evidence of disloyalty.

The Illinois Broyles Law, requiring state and public school employees to take a loyalty oath is one of the most thoroughgoing state acts on this subject. Similar legislation exists in Maryland, Pennsylvania, Texas and Washington. A Communist registration law operates in Wyoming. Loyalty oaths for particular occupations exist in other states: persons holding insurance licenses (District of Columbia); public accountants (New York); persons eligible for unemployment compensation (Ohio); wrestlers and prize-fighters (Indiana); students in state universities (Texas). California imposes an oath requirement on persons and organizations enjoying tax exemption. In general, the states have relaxed the "loyalty oath" fad of the 1950's.

LEGISLATIVE INVESTIGATIONS: Probably the most highly publicized aspect of the loyalty program has been the legislative investigations into subversion in various areas of American society. The House and Senate Committees on Un-American Activities are the best known of the legislative investigative committees, but in many of the states, parallel legislative investigative committees also exist. In civil liberties terms, these investigations, too often conducted in an atmosphere of political aggrandizement for the chairman of the committee, have posed two issues. The first is the highly dramatic issue of invoking the privilege against self-incrimination of the Fifth Amendment. (Discussed below. p. 44). The second is the more technical but equally significant issue of the permissible scope of congressional investigations.

The Supreme Court has ruled that the Un-American Activities Committee exceeded its jurisdiction in trying to compel a witness to name friends he had known as Communists. It held that the inquiry had strayed from the purpose of obtaining information for legislation and had no clear intent. The Court characterized the committee's powers as "excessively broad."

In actuality, the laws authorizing the House Committee on Un-American Activities confine its investigations to propaganda that is "subversive," "un-American," and "attacks the principle of the form of government as guaranteed by our Constitution." In the ordinary peacetime construction of these terms, the Committee would be limited

31

in its investigations to propaganda advocating the overthrow of the government of the United States. The Committee has never so limited itself, and Congress has never applied any limitations. In the *Watkins* case, the Court stepped in to provide the limitations and to remind legislative committees that the legitimate bounds of their activity is fact-finding for legislation. The Court specifically condemned the role of these committees as one of "exposure."

Yet, if civil libertarians had been moved by the *Watkins* decision to think that the powers of the HUAC had been substantially blunted, they learned in 1961 in the companion *Wilkerson* and *Barenblatt* cases where, in 5-4 decisions, the Court upheld contempt of Congress convictions, that considerations of national security might still outweigh the protection of the First Amendment. In those cases, witnesses before the HUAC had refused to answer the charge that they were members of the Communist Party.

The Impact on Civil Liberties of Loyalty-Security Machinery

The operation of loyalty-security programs, the administration of loyalty oaths and the conduct of legislative investigations have posed a number of major civil liberties issues. The extent, for example, to which the requirements of due process should be met in departmental or legislative hearings, is one such issue. This will be discussed at length in connection with the analysis of due process in Chapter II. It can be noted here, however, that the loss of employment and reputation, stemming from a loyalty hearing or a legislative investigation, while not a criminal penalty within the purview of the Fifth Amendment, is, in effect, a "punishment" of the individual concerned. Increasingly, the Supreme Court and students of loyalty-security machinery are coming to accept this reasoning and to provide for increased protection for the rights of individuals to a fair hearing.

The privilege against self-incrimination, contained in the Fifth Amendment (also discussed below at p. 44), has been one of the most dramatic civil liberties issues posed by legislative investigations. Invoking the privilege has generally been associated in the public mind with guilt of subversion, with the result that, although an individual may protect himself against criminal prosecution by pleading the privilege, he may be destroyed economically and socially by public opinion.

The particular civil liberties issue which relates to the First Amendment is that of "guilt by association," a doctrine which involves the judging of an individual on no other basis than his membership in a particular organization. Thus, mere membership is not sufficient to disqualify. A man's associations *are* evidence of his views, but not necessarily conclusive evidence. The Supreme Court has sought to modify the doctrine of "guilt by association" by reading into state loyalty oath legislation a requirement that the individual barred from public employment *knowingly* is or has been a member of a proscribed organization. Thus, mere membership is not sufficient to disqualify. There must be proof that the barred person knew the nature and purpose of the organization at the time of his membership.

An important aspect of the civil liberties problem is one that is actually beyond the reach of law. To an impressive extent, private groups, some of a vigilante character, have taken upon themselves the task of "exposure." Too often, these groups do not respect even the elementary requirements of due process and civil liberty, with the result that completely innocent individuals find themselves "blacklisted" from employment by employers who dare not defy the implied suggestion that "named" individuals are not "fit" for employment.

This aspect of private pressure is particularly manifest in privately endowed colleges, where the issue of academic freedom is involved. To a large extent, both educators and students have found themselves restrained in the expression of views, basic to an effective learning process, for fear that the expression of an "offensive" view or one subject to misinterpretation might jeopardize their careers.

Notwithstanding the seriousness of these implied threats to civil liberty, since 1954, there has been an observable trend toward greater respect for the rights of the individual in the administration of loyalty-security programs. Many of the excesses of the late forties and the period of the highwater mark of the late Senator Joseph P. McCarthy have been substantially rectified. While much of this is due to the Supreme Court, particularly since the advent of Chief Justice Earl Warren, the legislature and the executive have likewise contributed to the changing climate.

Chapter Two

PERSONAL LIBERTY

The essence of democracy is not only the right to freedom of expression, but also the knowledge that one's personal liberty cannot be disturbed except by "due process of law." Accordingly, the founding fathers wrote into the Articles of the Constitution and into the Bill of Rights a basic code of justice, protecting the individual against arbitrary action by government.

These guarantees of personal liberty include: (1) the privilege of the writ of habeas corpus (Article I, section 9); (2) protection against unreasonable searches and seizures (Fourth Amendment); (3) freedom from prosecution for serious crimes except by indictment or presentment by grand jury (Fifth Amendment); (4) the right to trial by jury in all criminal cases (Sixth Amendment); (5) the right to assistance of counsel (Sixth Amendment); (6) the right not to be a witness against onesself (Fifth Amendment); (7) the right to a fair trial consistent with due process of law (Fifth Amendment); (8) freedom from double jeopardy, i.e. no more than one criminal prosecution for the same offense (Sixth Amendment); (9) protection against excessive bail and fines and against cruel and unusual punishment (Eighth Amendment).

We have seen that the guarantees of the First Amendment, protecting freedom of expression against action by the federal government, apply equally and totally to the states by force of the Fourteenth Amendment. This is not true of the guarantees of personal liability.

For example, the provisions of the Fifth Amendment requiring criminal prosecution to be instituted by indictment or presentment by a grand jury is a constitutional requirement in federal courts only. A state prosecution instituted by information—where the District Attorney or the Attorney General, rather than a grand jury, makes the accusation—is valid. Likewise, many of the states dispense with jury trial in minor criminal cases, and the right to counsel in criminal cases is more extensive in federal courts than in state courts. Again, the protection against unreasonable searches and seizures, provided in the Fourth Amendment, operates differently under federal rules of evidence than under state procedures. The situation has been summarized by Justice Felix Frankfurter:

"In an impressive body of decisions this Court has decided that the Due Process Clause of the Fourteenth Amendment expresses a demand for civilized standards which are not defined by the specifically enumerated guarantees of the Bill of Rights. they neither contain the particularities of the first eight amendments nor are they confined to them."

Habeas Corpus—Article I. Section 9

"The Constitution of the United States originally contained no bill of rights. It did, however, protect civil liberty by a few scattered clauses. Five of these clauses listed things which the new federal government might not do. It could not, save in time of rebellion or acute public danger, suspend the writ of *habeas corpus*, the traditional safeguard against unjust imprisonment. It could pass no bill of attainder, a conviction and punishment for a crime by legislative act rather than by judicial process. It could pass no *ex post facto* law, that is, it could not, by passing a new law, make the position of persons accused of crime, less favorable than when the crime was committed. It could not deny to those who broke its laws a trial by jury. And finally, it could punish for treason only under carefully defined restrictions.

"Three other clauses protected civil liberty from state interference. No state might pass a bill of attainder; it could not pass an *ex post facto* law; it could pass no law impairing the obligation of contracts. In addition, the states were directed to give to the citizens of each state the privileges and immunities of citizens in the several states. This was to prevent the citizen of a state from being treated like a foreigner when he went into other states." (from New Threats to American Freedoms, by Robert Cushman, Public Affairs Pamphlet No. 143).

Of all these guarantees of personal liberty that predated the Bill of Rights, the most important is the privilege of the writ of *habeas corpus*. This is a writ by which a person who is being restrained of his liberty may secure a determination by a judge whether such restraint is proper. On hearing, the judge will generally limit himself to the question whether the detaining authority had jurisdiction. In a case arising during the Civil War, the Supreme Court held that a writ may be suspended only when martial law has been declared and the courts are actually closed. Mere existence of a state of war is insufficient to justify suspension of the writ.

Habeas corpus is not a substitute for an appeal, but is limited only to those situations in which the individual has no other means of judicial review. For example, an alien who is detained for deportation may sue out a writ of *habeas corpus* to have a judicial review of the legality of his detention.

In recent years, the Supreme Court has broadened the scope of the writ. It is now considered an appropriate remedy where a conviction in a state court has been in disregard of the constitutional right of the accused, and where the writ is the only effective means of preserving all his rights. Wrongful failure to provide counsel to an accused in a criminal case is a sufficient basis to warrant review of conviction on *habeas corpus.* The reasoning behind this is that where constitutional rights are violated, a court loses jurisdiction in the course of a trial. On the other hand, the Supreme Court has also held that where an individual's rights can be completely protected through appeal, he cannot fail to appeal his conviction and then subsequently bring *habeas corpus* to question the legality of his detention.

Searches and Seizures—The Fourth Amendment

The people have the right to be secure in their persons, houses, papers and effects against unreasonable searches and seizures. Warrants shall issue only on probable cause and shall describe the place to be searched and the persons or things to be seized. So states the Fourth Amendment.

In general, an officer can make an arrest only with a warrant. If a crime is committed in his presence, however, an officer can make an arrest on the spot without a warrant. An officer may not, however, conduct a search without a warrant and then make an arrest on the basis of what he finds. Under these circumstances, the search, the seizure and the arrest are all unlawful.

Following a lawful arrest, the officer has the right to search the person of the prisoner and to seize those articles found on his person which are connected with the crime. The articles seized may be either the instruments of the crime, i.e. a gun in a robbery, or the spoils of the crime, i.e. stolen jewels. The officer may not seize papers which are evidence of the crime without a warrant.

In the absence of a warrant, the premises in which the prisoner is taken into custody may not be searched. However, visible articles which are the instruments of the crime may be seized, where there has not been sufficient time for the officer to secure a warrant. During Prohibition, for example, the police were privileged to seize bootlegged liquor in automobiles without a warrant, the courts taking into consideration the fact that a car could make a speedy getaway before a warrant could be secured. But the seizure of illegal distilling apparatus without a warrant, although incident to a lawful arrest, was held invalid, where there had been sufficient time to procure a warrant.

For a search warrant to be issued, there must be more than suspicion of crime. A warrant will issue only upon probable cause. Moreover, it must describe specifically the premises to be searched. "Fishing expeditions" and general ransacking of a person's home are forbidden whether the officer acts under the authority of a warrant or without one.

On the other hand, the right of search and seizure with or without warrant is broadened where the articles seized are government property, such as gasoline ration coupons or draft cards. The Supreme Court has affirmed the conviction of a person for illegal possession of draft cards which the arresting officer turned up after a five hour search of the defendant's home. The search warrant had specified only checks allegedly used by the defendant in a series of forgeries. In other words, the court affirmed conviction for a crime which had been uncovered only as a result of a search not specifically authorized by the search warrant. The Court appeared to be impressed by the fact that draft cards are government property.

In a subsequent case where government property was not involved, the Court retreated from this position, reversing the conviction of a woman who had been arrested without a warrant for conducting an opium den. The conviction was based on the opium which the officers discovered in her hotel room after a limited search. The Court held that there had been ample time for the officers to procure both a warrant for her arrest and a warrant to search her premises.

The Fourth Amendment does not protect the right of privacy generally. Thus, the interesting question frequently arises, "when is a search not a search?" If an officer uncovers evidence by eavesdropping, he is violating the right of privacy; but the courts have held that he is not violating the Fourth Amendment because he is not trespassing on the person, home, papers or effects of the individual involved. In short, he is not engaged in a "search" within the meaning of the Fourth Amendment. Whenever an officer uncovers crime through his senses, aided or unaided by mechanical gadgets—smell (bootlegged liquor, opium); hearing (eavesdropping, wire tapping, detectaphones); sight (peeping)—the Fourth Amendment is not violated. It is only a trespass on the person or property or access to person or property by fraud or trick that is forbidden by the Fourth Amendment.

WIRETAPPING: While the Supreme Court has held that the practice does not violate the Fourth Amendment, it has also held that the Federal Communications Act of 1934 forbids it. Legislation is pending in Congress that would permit federal wiretapping without a court order. Under the measure, the Attorney General would be empowered to issue wiretap orders in national security cases suuch as espionage, treason, sedition, subversive activities and unauthorized disclosure of atomic information. The bill also calls for court-authorized wiretapping by federal agents in investigations of murder, kidnapping, gambling and narcotics.

Some 33 states also have laws which forbid wiretapping, but many of them exempt police officers. In New York, a police officer is permitted to tap wires only by warrant which issues where there are reasonable grounds to believe that evidence of crime may thus be obtained. The warrant must specify the means of communication to be tapped and must name the person or persons whose communications are to be intercepted and the purpose of the interception. Many experts of criminal and constitutional law have recommended the New York rule to the federal authorities.

Wiretapping brings into focus the difference between the federal government and the states on the question of the admissibility of evidence uncovered by unlawful searches and seizures. Under the Fifth Amendment, an individual has the right not to be a witness against himself. The federal courts have held that to permit evidence that is uncovered through unlawful searches and seizures or through other illegal methods to be introduced on trial would violate the privilege against self-incrimination. The federal rule, therefore, bars as evidence any matter that results from unlawful searchc or seizure. Since wiretapping is unlawful under the federal law, evidence secured by wiretapping is inadmissible in federal courts. Note, however, that evidence unlawfully secured by a state officer is admissible in federal court unless the state officer worked with federal officers or acted as their agents.

The state rules operate quite differently. In the first place, neither the Fourth Amendment nor the privilege against self-incrimination contained in the Fifth Amendment are binding on the states. Accordingly, most of the states follow the common law rule that an unlawful search or seizure furnishes only the basis of a civil or criminal action against the offending officer. They admit into evidence matter which has been secured by unlawful search or seizure. The theory behind this rule is that neither the guilty defendant nor the over-zealous officer escapes punishment. The federal rule has been criticized on the grounds that it frequently permits a guilty defendant to go free and in no way punishes an offending officer.

Not every defendant who is convicted on evidence that has been obtained illegally can invoke the protection of the Fourth Amendment. If there is any suggestion of consent to search and seizure on the part of the defendant, he cannot subsequently challenge its legality even though it would have been unlawful had he not consented. Moreover to invoke the Fourth Amendment, a defendant must be the direct and immediate victim of the unlawful search and seizure. Thus, if tapping the telephone conversations of A and B furnishes evidence of crime committed by C, C cannot secure a reversal of his conviction by resort to the Fourth Amendment.

Prosecution Without Persecution—The Fifth Amendment

INDICTMENT BY GRAND JURY: The Fifth Amendment requires that prosecution for all "capital or infamous crimes" be instituted by indictment or presentment by a grand jury. The requirement has been held not to apply to the states, although most states have similar provisions in their state constitutions. In some states, like Louisiana and California, prosecution may be begun by information, i.e. the District Attorney or Attorney General, rather than the grand jury, makes a sworn accusation that the defendant has committed a crime. Michigan has a "one man" grand jury system under which a judge sitting as a grand jury may indict. The same judge who acts as a grand jury may not subsequently preside at the trial.

As to the specific crimes for which indictment is required, they are capital crimes—those which carry the death penalty as punishment—and infamous crimes—those which are punished either by imprisonment in a state penitentiary (as distinguished from a workhouse or county jail) or by sentence to hard labor. Where neither a peni-

41

tentiary term nor hard labor sentence is involved in the punishment, grand jury indictment is not required.

The Fifth Amendment lists certain exceptions to the requirement of indictment by a grand jury. Army or Navy personnel, accused of committing a capital or infamous crime, need not be indicted by a grand jury; likewise a member of the militia in time of war or public danger. During the Second World War, the Supreme Court decided that persons in the service of the enemy, although not expressly excepted by the language of the Fifth Amendment, need not be indicted by a grand jury but can be dealt with in accordance with military law by a military tribunal.

As to whether a person may waive the right to indictment or presentment by a grand jury, the courts have generally upheld the validity of state statutes authorizing waiver even where the state constitutions guarantee grand jury indictment. New York, however, has ruled that indictment is necessary to give a court jurisdiction to proceed and that a statute authorizing waiver of indictment is unconstitutional.

DOUBLE JEOPARDY: The Fifth Amendment likewise prevents any person from being tried more than once for the same offense. This provision, like most of the guarantees of personal liberty, applies to the federal government only. However, except for Connecticut, Maryland, Massachusetts, North Carolina and Vermont, each of the state constitutions likewise incorporates this protection.

The major issue in securing this right is the definition of a "first jeopardy." For one thing, it is clear that this provision does not prevent a state from punishing a person for the very same conduct which is also a federal offense. During the Prohibition era, many persons were brought to book under both federal and state laws. Similarly, a criminal prosecution does not bar a civil action and vice-versa.

Where a verdict is reached. As a general rule, it is not double jeopardy to prosecute twice for the same conduct, so long as the crimes are different. Crimes are different unless the evidence required to sustain both is the same. Conviction or acquittal of a crime which includes lesser offenses will generally bar prosecution for the lesser offense. Thus, if a man is prosecuted for rape, he cannot on acquittal be prosecuted for assault with intent to rape. Similarly, conviction or acquittal for a lesser offense bars prosecution for the greater offense which includes it. If a man is convicted of assault with intent to rape, he cannot then be prosecuted for rape. In like manner, prosecution for battery has been held to bar prosecution for attempted rape; prosecution for assault with intent to kill bars prosecution for mayhem; prosecution for petty larceny bars prosecution for robbery.

Where, however, after the first prosecution, a new circumstance, changing the criminal character of the defendant's conduct arises, the defendant may be prosecuted for the greater offense. Assume that a man is convicted of assault with intent to kill, and subsequently, his victim in fact dies, the death being traceable to the assault. The defendant, may then be prosecuted for homicide. This is not double jeopardy since, on the first trial, the victim still being alive, the defendant could not have been prosecuted for homicide.

There is even the possibility of prosecution for homicide under these circumstances if the defendant is initially acquitted of assault with intent to kill. For in many states, i.e. Illinois, homicide other than murder in the first degree does not require intent to kill, and so a man might not be guilty of assault with intent to kill and still be guilty of homicide if his victim subsequently dies.

Where a lower court verdict is appealed, reversal of a defendant's conviction does not bar a new trial. However, when the prosecution appeals an acquittal, the majority of states will deny a new trial regardless of errors committed by the trial court.

Before verdict is reached. In interpreting the double jeopardy provision, the courts have laid down the general rule that one is in jeopardy when put upon trial before a court of competent jurisdiction, upon an indictment sufficient to sustain a conviction, and a jury has been impanelled and sworn to try him. Where a person is tried under an indictment so defective that conviction will have to be reversed for error, he may be indicted again. In like manner, a refusal of a grand jury to indict or the quashing of a proceeding prior to impaneling a jury will not bar subsequent indictment and prosecution.

But once the jury is impanelled, there being no defects in the indictment, the defendant is placed in "first jeopardy." Unless the defense subsequently requests a continuance (postponement) or some urgent necessity stops the trial prior to verdict of conviction or acquittal, any termination prior to verdict will be deemed a bar to a new trial. Urgent necessity sufficient to dispose of the claim of double jeopardy and permit a new trial has been found in the following situations: when the term of court ends before a decision is reached, when the jury is unable to agree within a reasonable time, when a biased judgment is feared, and when persons essential to the proper completion of the trial are excusably absent, i. e. a juror or the judge takes ill. The courts, however, have generally refused to find that absence of the prosecution's witnesses constitutes urgent necessity.

Sentence and Punishment. Double jeopardy may arise in the sentencing of a defendant. Where a judge ordered payment of a fine, he was held debarred from imposing a prison sentence after the fine had been tendered to the court. The statute in question gave the court the power to fine or to imprison but not both.

With reference to double jeopardy in punishment, perhaps the most spectacular case ever to arise involved the unsuccessful electrocution of a convicted Negro in Louisiana. The first electrocution having failed, the Supreme Court held that it was neither double jeopardy nor cruel and unusual punishment to attempt a second electrocution.

THE PRIVILEGE AGAINST SELF-INCRIMINATION: "I refuse to answer on grounds that it may incriminate or degrade me" is a response which is not available to witnesses with the regularity that one might suppose. As previously observed, the right not to be a witness against oneself, as laid down in the Fifth Amendment, does not bind the states, and insistence by a state court that a person giving incriminating testimony will not be reviewed by the Supreme Court. Among the states, however, all constitutions except those of Iowa and New Jersey afford protection both on the federal and state levels. A question put to a witness in federal court which may uncover evidence of state crime is not protected, nor is a question asked in a state court which may uncover violation of a federal law.

While the governing clause of the Fifth Amendment reads "no person shall be compelled in *any criminal case* to be a witness against himself," the courts have applied the privilege against self-incrimination to any proceeding where a witness may incriminate himself by answering a question or giving testimony. Thus, the privilege applies not only in criminal proceedings, but in grand jury investigations, bankruptcy proceedings, statutory proceedings for forfeiture of goods, and even in civil suits where an aswer to a question might tend to establish the witness' criminal liability. Where the privilege operates, it is improper for a federal judge to comment on a refusal to testify, but it is not improper for a state judge to do so. In no case, however, may a judge charge that refusal to testify creates a presumption of guilt.

The privilege applies to both oral and written testimony. However, there are a number of situations where the privilege cannot be invoked. Corporations are not protected by the privilege, and the records of a corporation may not be withheld by its officers. Similarly, a public official cannot refuse to produce the public records in his custody.

A fundamental question that has been increasingly posed in recent years is whether the privilege protects private business records required to be kept by statute or administrative regulation. Although the Supreme Court has not yet directly considered the problem, a majority of lower federal courts have held that such records are of a "quasi-public" nature, and therefore beyond the scope of the privilege against self-incrimination. Under these decisions, if a regulation is otherwise valid, it will not be unconstitutional for requiring records to be kept and subsequently produced, even though they may reveal evidence of crime.

Another problem that has become increasingly important in recent years is the operation of the privilege against self-incrimination at legislative investigations. The effect of pleading the Fifth on the reputation of witness, and his consequent punishment by public opinion have been considered earlier. (see p. 33). There seems to be no doubt that the privilege applies. The issue is whether the privilege can be removed by the operation of an immunity statute, i. e. a statute which protects a witness from criminal prosecution on the basis of his testimony. The Supreme Court has held that an immunity statute merely providing protection against subsequent use of a witness' testimony as evidence in a criminal prosecution against him is insufficient to prevent the operation of the privilege against self-incrimination. Under such a statute, the testimony might furnish clues by which other evidence of crime could be uncovered, and the witness could then be prosecuted on the basis of such evidence. On the other hand, a statute which grants a witness total immunity from criminal prosecution as to any matter concerning which he testifies has been deemed sufficient to suspend the operation of the privilege against self-incrimination. Such legislation is the Federal Immunity Statute of 1954, which the Supreme Court held valid in 1956.

The privilege against self-incrimination may be waived, and this frequently becomes an important issue in court proceedings. A witness will be answering a series of questions and suddenly find himself confronted with the prospect of confessing to a crime if he answers the next question. The courts have held that the privilege is waived where the witness, by answering some questions, leads himself to the point where the incriminating question is asked. He is expected to foresee the logical course of questioning, and to invoke his privilege early in the testimony.

DUE PROCESS: The reader will observe that most of the guarantees of personal liberty contained in the Bill of Rights are not carried over into the Fourteen Amendment. The legal reasoning behind this has been the fact that both the Fifth and Fourteenth Amendments contain identically worded "due process" clauses, and that therefore due process under the Fourteenth Amendment can mean no more than it means under the Fifth Amendment. While in many ways the due process clause of the Fourteenth Amendment has grown to the stature of a second Bill of Rights, particularly in its protection of freedom of expression, in terms of personal liberty, it has come to mean only "fair trial," the same meaning which it has under the Fifth Amendment.

What are the elements of due process? In the first place, due process requires that a person receive notice of charge or claim against him and that, on demand, he be furnished with a bill of particulars specifying the exact nature of such charge or claim. Secondly, due process requires an atmosphere in which a fair hearing can be conducted. There is no "fair trial" where mob feeling is such that lynching is threatened if a prisoner is not convicted. There is no "fair trial" where the judge is prejudiced or where the jury is improperly chosen, i. e. Negroes have been deliberately excluded from jury service where a Negro is on trial. Thirdly, confessions extorted by third degree methods or by fraud and trickery are inconsistent with due process as is perjured testimony. The presence either of extorted confessions or of perjured testimony will require reversal of a conviction regardless of other evidence in the case.

Due process does not include the right to appeal, except that there must be a provision for judicial review where constitutional issues are involved, i. e. by writ of *habeas corpus*. However, where a state has created an appeals machinery, to deprive a person of an appeal is a violation of due process as well as a denial of equal protection of the laws.

Of all the guarantees of personal liberty, due process is probably the most elastic, since it can be made to cover all situations in which minimum standards of fair hearing have not been maintained. Thus, while other guarantees of the Bill of Rights are not expressly binding on the states, if a state acts with wanton disregard of these guarantees, thereby prejudicing the defendant, the proceeding can be set aside as wanting in due process. This is particularly true where the right to trial by jury and to assistance of counsel under the Sixth Amendment is involved.

One of the most important issues of the post-war period has been the applicability of requirements of due process to loyalty hearings. Under one approach, it is argued that there is no "right" to a federal job, and that loss of a government job is not "punishment" in the legal sense. From this premise it follows that the requirements of due process as they apply to a court trial have no applicability to a hearing to determine the suitability of an individual for federal employment. As late as 1950, the Supreme Court upheld this point of view—although by a margin no greater than a 4-4 split which upheld a 2-1 decision of a lower federal court.

It was not until 1955 that the Court began to reexamine this line of thinking and to extend due process requirements to hearings under loyalty-security executive orders. Actually, in *Peters* v. *Hobby*, decided that year, the majority decision avoided the constitutional issue of due process and ordered the reinstatement of Dr. Peters on the grounds that the loyalty review board had exceeded its authority, when it reversed a departmental decision sustaining Dr. Peters' loyalty. The concurring decision by Justice Douglas, however, came to grips with the problem of due process.

In the *Jencks* case, (1957), the Court held that defendants in criminal cases have the right to examine F.B.I. reports of witnesses who testify against them. This has been variously interpreted in lower courts as meaning the handing over of full investigative reports to defense counsel, sometimes even in advance of going to trial.

The Attorney General and the Director of the F.B.I. have both taken the position that this decision threatens a breakdown in Federal law enforcement through the compelled exposure of confidential informants and methods of procedure, particularly in counter-espionage cases. The 85th Congress has sought to set limits to the Court's decision through legislation protecting the files of the F.B.I. and other Federal agencies from public exposure.

The cases since *Peters* seem to indicate that in the loyalty-security area, the Court will review each case on its own factual situation and will not attempt an all-encompassing rule of law. In the *Greene* case (1959), the security firing of a government engineer was reversed because he had not received a full due process hearing. Yet in *Brawner* (1960), the Court said, "The Fifth Amendment does not require a trial-type hearing in every conceivable case of government impairment of interest."

In a totally different area, the Supreme Court in the *Dixon* case (1962) upheld a lower court decision that the expulsion of six Alabama State College students for sit-in activities was an unconstitutional act on the part of the tax-supported college in the absence of a hearing. This would appear to suggest that, in connection with the overall assertion of civil rights (see ahead, Chapter Three) protections afforded by the First, Fifth and Fourteenth Amendments will take precedence over the so-called police power and public welfare, while in the area of national security, though the equation of the early forties has been somewhat restored, national security will probably continue to enjoy some precedence over individual freedom.

Trial and Defense—The Sixth Amendment

TRIAL BY JURY: The Sixth Amendment requires a speedy and public trial by an impartial jury in the district in which the crime has occurred. This requirement of jury trial applies to the federal government but is not binding on the states, and many of the states dispense with jury trial in prosecutions for minor crimes and misdemeanors.

All of the states, however, have constitutional provisions requiring trial by jury for serious crimes.

As to whether trial by jury may be waived, the courts have gradually moved away from their former unyielding insistence on trial by jury where serious crimes are involved. With reference to the federal courts, the Supreme Court has held that partial waiver of jury, in the sense of agreement by defense and prosecution on less than twelve jurors sitting in a criminal case, is permissible. The language in this case has been used by state courts to validate statutes authorizing complete waiver of trial by jury notwithstanding the requirements of state constitutions. New York, by constitutional amendment, authorizes the waiver of trial by jury in all cases where it is agreeable to defense and prosecution.

The more important issue in connection with trial by jury is the requirement that the jury be impartial. For, while trial by jury, in and of itself, is not regarded as an essential element of due process, trial by an *impartial* jury is a different matter. A partisan or prejudiced jury, or one drawn from lists which exclude certain persons solely because of their race, class or sex, is a denial of due process and forbidden by the Fifth and Fourteenth Amendments to the Constitution.

The Supreme Court has indicated that it thinks that an impartial jury should be one chosen from a cross-section of the population. However, the Constitution does not secure to an accused person the right to have his race represented on the jury that indicts or tries him. It is only the deliberate exclusion from the jury lists of Negroes, laborers or women that is a violation of due process and a denial of equal protection of the laws. Accordingly, when the prosecution rejects all Negroes on the jury list, in the exercise of its privilege to reject up to twenty jurors without giving any reason, the courts have held that this is not a violation of due process.

This raises the problem of the legality of so-called "blue ribbon" juries, i. e. juries selected from lists composed of persons presumed to be more competent, more intelligent and less prejudiced than ordinary jurors. "Blue ribbon" juries are legal in eight states—Alabama, Michigan (Detroit only), New Jersey, New York (New York City only), Tennessee (civil cases only), Vermont, Virginia (civil cases only).

In most states where it is permitted, a "blue ribbon" jury may be granted on motion of either party where the court is convinced that the importance or intricacy of the case or the demands of efficient and impartial justice require it. In other words, the granting or denial of a "blue ribbon" jury is almost wholly discretionary with the trial court.

In New York, the "blue ribbon" jury is picked from the list of ordinary jurors by the county clerk. Each juror is personally interviewed and required to swear that he has no scruples against the death penalty, no such preformed opinion that he is unable to lay it aside, and no prejudice against particular laws or defenses. In a recent case before the Supreme Court, two labor leaders charged with extortion challenged the validity of the New York "blue ribbon" jury system on the grounds that workers and women had been purposely excluded from the jury lists and that "blue ribbon" juries have a greater tendency to convict than do ordinary juries.

In a split decision, the Court upheld the "blue ribbon" jury, deciding that it is neither a violation of due process nor a denial of equal protection of the laws. The Court found no deliberate or systematic exclusion of workers, and found nothing wrong with the New York rule permitting women to claim exemption from both ordinary and "blue ribbon" juries.

Actually, the uniformly higher quality of ordinary juries is gradually outdating the "blue ribbon" jury. Pennsylvania abolished its "blue ribbon" jury system in 1937, and Massachusetts defeated a bill that would have authorized "blue ribbon" juries. New York, by a recent statutory amendment, set the same qualifications for ordinary jurors as for "blue ribbon" jurors.

ADVICE OF COUNSEL: "Say nothing until you talk

to me!" is the first advice of the criminal lawyer to his client who has just been booked on criminal charges. A person accused of crime, where he can afford counsel, will spare no expense to get the best lawyer in town. For, he recognizes that a good lawyer is his best protection. Yet, a great number of persons charged with crime, ranging all the way from minor offenses to first degree murder, are often too poor to engage the services of a lawyer and too ignorant to defend themselves properly. What protection does our system of justice offer these people?

"In all criminal prosecutions, the accuser shall enjoy the right . . . to have the assistance of counsel for his defense." So reads the Sixth Amendment to the Constitution which, like the other guarantees of personal liberty, applies only to the federal government. This means that any person charged with the commission of a crime under federal laws is entitled to a lawyer. No distinction is made between capital crimes—those for which the death sentence is the penalty—and non-capital crimes. In fact, even minor offenses under federal laws have been held to require the appointment of counsel for a defendant who is unable to pay for legal services.

The right to counsel in state courts is not as extensive as in federal courts. In all capital cases, the rule is the same. Whether there is a state statute or not, the court must appoint counsel to represent a defendant where the penalty on conviction will be death and the defendant is unable to supply counsel of his own. In noncapital cases, however, the federal rule is not applicable to the states.

Where there is a state statute, the state court is required to follow it. Statutes requiring that indigent defendants in noncapital as well as capital criminal cases be provided with counsel on request exist in 25 states—Arizona, Arkansas, California, Idaho, Illinois, Iowa, Kansas, Louisiana, Minnesota, Missouri, Montana, Nebraska, Nevada, New Hampshire, New Jersey, New York, North Dakota, Ohio, Oklahoma, Oregon, South Dakota, Tennessee, Utah, Washington and Wyoming. Georgia and Kentucky require appointment of counsel in all criminal cases by constitutional amendment. In Connecticut, Florida, Indiana, Michigan, Pennsylvania, Virginia, West Virginia and Wisconsin, court decisions have established the requirement that in all felonies or criminal cases punishable by imprisonment in a penitentiary or by imprisonment for several years, indigent defendants must be provided with counsel on request.

In Alabama, Mississippi, Maryland and Texas, the right to counsel in noncapital cases has been totally rejected. In Colorado, Delaware, Maine, Massachusetts, New Mexico, North Carolina, Rhode Island, South Carolina and Vermont, there are no set rules. In these states, the right to counsel will depend on whether the absence of counsel will so prejudice the conduct of defendant's trial that it cannot be said to be a "fair trial," and therefore violates due process.

Thus, in noncapital cases, a defendant seeking to establish the unconstitutionality of his conviction on the grounds that defense counsel was not appointed, must show that either in view of the seriousness of the charge against him or the complicated legal issues involved, or his youth and ignorance, or the bias or error of the trial judge, the absence of counsel so prejudiced him that the trial did not square with "common and fundamental ideas of fairness." In the absence of these prejudicial factors, it has been held that a state court need not ask the accused whether he desires counsel, nor wether he can procure counsel, nor need the court assign counsel if the accused is unrepresented.

But even where the right to counsel is established, there are still questions as to the extent of the protection afforded. The following general conclusions may be stated: (1) Even if the accused desires to plead guilty at arraignment, he must be advised of his right to counsel both in the federal courts and in those states which require the appointment of counsel. Moreover, a plea of guilty is not in itself a waiver of the right to counsel but may be introduced as evidence of waiver. Thus, a defendant who has pleaded guilty and has not had the benefit of counsel at any stage of the proceeding may attack his conviction on the grounds that he was not represented by counsel, so long as he can prove that he did not waive his right. If he can prove that at the time he pleaded guilty, he was insane, under the influence of drugs, deaf, ignorant of his rights or influenced by coercion or false promise, it will not be said that he waived his right to counsel.

(2) The right to counsel means effective assistance of counsel and requires that counsel be competent, that there be opportunity to confer privately with and receive the advice of one's counsel, that there be opportunity for counsel adequate to prepare the defense, and that there be opportunity for counsel to present the case without interference or prejudice.

(3) As to whether counsel is required to be present at all stages of a proceeding, in capital cases, the courts have leaned to the rule that regardless of whether or not the accused has been prejudiced by the absence of counsel either at arraignment, trial or sentence, absence at any one stage is a deprivation of the right to counsel. In noncapital cases, however, the courts have looked to the issue of whether or not the accused was actually prejudiced by the absence of counsel. In New York, for example, the absence of counsel at arraigment has been held to be cured by counsel's subsequent presence at the trial or on the day of sentence. Likewise, where counsel's withdrawal before verdict was found to cause no prejudice to the accused, absence of counsel did not void the proceeding. In general, it is most important for counsel to be present at sentence, in order to take advantage either of a motion for a new trial, an appeal or a request for leniency in sentence.

OTHER RIGHTS OF DEFENSE: Under the Sixth Amendment, a defendant has the right to be confronted with the witnesses against him and to have compulsory process (subpoena) to bring forth the witnesses in his favor. On trial, both the prosecution and the defense have the right to cross-examine each other's witnesses. As previously noted (see p. 48), this issue has been involved in loyalty hearings.

The Eighth Amendment protects a person charged with crime from excessive bail and fine and from cruel and unusual punishment. While, in general, the courts will not review the figure at which bail is set, discrimination by federal officers in the setting of bail or fine is forbidden.

Conclusion

In making a reality of the guarantees of personal liberty contained in the Bill of Rights and of the due process clause of the Fourteenth Amendment, the state courts and the United States Supreme Court have had the problem of pointing a path to freedom for those who are the victims of ignorance and injustice while, at the same time, not opening the gates of our jails for hardened criminals. The growing tendency is to view each case on its particular facts, to ascertain whether fundamental concepts of justice and fairness have governed. While this approach makes for some uncertainty in the administration of law, it is perhaps the surest way to protect both the rights of the accused and the rights of the community. The one recent development to be pointed out is the trend toward applying the requirements of fair trial to the twilight area of legislative investigations and loyalty hearings even though these are not precisely criminal in nature. Additionally, it is suggested that, in connection with the assertion, legally and defacto, of civil rights, unique interpretations of the First, Fifth and Fourteenth Amendments will emanate from the Supreme Court, the effect of which will be to buttress social action in behalf of civil rights. This is reminiscent of a generation ago when the rights of organized labor became similarly involved with such issues as freedom of expression as justification for picket lines. Today, it is freedom of expression that gives legal justification to the sit-in. These matters are further reviewed in the ensuing chapter.

Chapter Three
CIVIL RIGHTS

May, 1964, marks the tenth anniversary of the momentous Supreme Court decision declaring segregation of the races in public schools unconstitutional. While this case is regarded as a milestone in the history of American constitutional law, it has been significant not only for itself, but for the fact that it ushered in a decade in which "civil rights" emerged as perhaps the most important social issue of our times. It has been a decade marked by significant court decisions and growing state legislation which has had the simultaneous effect of expanding the legal structure of civil rights protection and eroding the legal structure of segregation. At the same time, social action techniques—boycotts, bus strikes, freedom rides, sit-ins—utilized to dramatize the fight for civil rights have themselves created legal issues involving the limitations on freedom of expression. Thus, considerations of civil rights and civil liberties have become increasingly paired, as was true a generation ago when the assertion of the rights of organized labor likewise produced a series of civil liberties issues, ranging from picket lines on the one side to employer free speech on the other.

I. THE ROLE OF THE FEDERAL GOVERNMENT

While the Congress has been grappling with civil rights legislation more far-reaching than anything enacted at the federal level in nearly a hundred years, the major responsibility for the protection of civil rights has fallen principally to the Supreme Court of the United States and to the legislatures of the states. The reason for this has been the fact that the power of the federal government is very strictly defined under the "Civil Rights" Amendments to the Constitution—the Thirteenth, Fourteenth and Fifteenth Amendments.

The Thirteenth Amendment abolishes slavery. The Fourteentth Amendment contains three specific prohibitions: (1) no state shall abridge the privileges and immunities of citizens of the United States; (2) no state shall deprive any person of life, liberty or property without due process of law; (3) no state shall deny to any person the equal protection of the laws. The Fifteenth Amendment assures that the right to vote shall not be denied or abridged by the United States or by any state on account of race, color or previous condition of servitude. While each Amendment empowers Congress to enact enforcing legislation, they also limit the power of the federal government to act. The Anti-Slavery Amendment (XIII) applies to the federal government, the states and private individuals alike; the Due Process Amendment (XIV) prohibits only state action; and the Vote Amendment (XV) prohibits only federal and state action. Thus, while violations of civil rights by state or federal officers may always be dealt with by federal action, *there are relatively few violations of civil rights by private individuals with which the federal government has power to deal.*

There is a history to this limitation of federal power. In 1875, the Congress passed "An Act to Protect All Citizens in Their Civil and Legal Rights." Under this Act, all persons were held entitled to the full and equal enjoyment of inns, public conveyances, theatres and other places of public amusement. Violation of the Act was a misdemeanor and provision was included for $500 civil damages to be paid by the offender to the person aggrieved.

About eight years after the adoption of this Civil Rights Act, the Supreme Court held it unconstitutional. The Court decided that the Fourteenth Amendment, under which the law had been passed, prohibited only invasions by the *states* of the rights of individuals, but not the invasion of those rights by other *individuals*. The Court declared that the regulation of the conduct of individuals toward one another on matters of civil rights was exclusively the job of the states and not the federal government.

These limitations become clearer upon examination of the major civil rights sections of federal legislation.

Section 241—Conspiracy to Violate the Rights of Citizens

Section 241 of Title 18 of the United States Code is directed against any two or more persons who conspire to interfere with a citizen in the exercise of rights or privileges guaranteed by the Constitution or laws of the United States. The penalty for violation is a fine of not more than $5,000 or imprisonment for not more than ten years or both.

This section seeks to protect a citizen (not merely a resident) against a conspiracy of individuals (they may be either private individuals, public officers or a combination of both) to deprive him of his constitutional rights. Actually, however, the rights and privileges of citizens that are guaranteed by the Constitution against interference by *private individuals* are few in number. They do not include such basic rights as freedom of speech, press, assembly and religious worship; due process of law; or equal protection of the laws. These rights are guaranteed by the Constitution only against governmental action. Thus, where private individuals are concerned, it would be only a conspiracy to deprive a citizen of his right to be free from slavery or involuntary servitude, or his rights as a citizen of the United States (as distinguished from his rights as a citizen of the state in which he resides) which is actionable.

Because of these limitations of coverage, and because this section requires proof of a conspiracy, it is seldom invoked in federal prosecutions. Peonage (forcing a person into involuntary servitude) is more effectively dealt with through the Anti-Peonage Act (Section 444, Title 18, U. S. Code) which covers individual as well as governmental action, and mob violence is beyond the constitutional reach of this section. Presumably, it protects rights created by federal legislation. But, thus far, the only such right clearly protected by Section 241 has been the right under the Homestead laws to make a homestead entry and hold the land. The Civil Rights Section of the Department of Justice has called attention to the possible use of Section 241 to protect rights and benefits stemming from the Social Security Act, the Fair Labor Standards Act, the National Labor Relations Act, acts conferring rights and benefits on the G. I. and the veterans housing acts, and agricultural acts.

Section 242—Denial of Rights under Color of Law

Section 242 of Title 18 is directed against any person who, *under color of law,* commits either of two offenses: (a) willfully denies to any inhabitant the rights and privileges guaranteed by the Constitution and federal laws; (b) willfully subjects any inhabitant, on account of his alienage, color or race to different punishments than are prescribed for the punishment of citizens. The section provides a fine of not more than $1,000 or imprisonment for not more than one year or both. This section, unlike Section 241, can be violated by a single person acting alone, so long as he acts under color of law. It cannot, however, be used against private individuals, whether acting singly or together.

The chief value of this section has been to deal with instances of police brutality—although, as pointed out by the Department of Justice, the relatively mild penalty is frequently out of proportion to the offense committed. The following types of conduct, amounting to police brutality, have been prosecuted under Section 242:

—— A law enforcement officer, uses third degree treat*ment* on an arrested suspect in order to extort a confession.

—— A law enforcement officer, operating a racket, causes the arrest and imprisonment of innocent people for purposes of extorting money from them.

—— A law enforcement officer, seeking to prevent a person from expressing his point of view, forces a large dose of castor oil down him, and then runs him out of town.

—— A law enforcement officer arrests a person, and then,

without trial, requires his prisoner to do forced labor on the officer's property.

—— A law enforcement officer uses his authority to make an arrest, and then kills his prisoner as part of a willful attempt to deprive him of a fair trial.

Section 242 is the only instrumentality available to the federal government to deal with lynchings. Up to the last few years, this was a serious problem since the southern states in which lynchings most often occurred, were the very states least willing to deal with them. More recently, however, not only has the number of lynchings declined sharply, but lynchings have been prosecuted by the states. Unwillingness of southern juries to convict white men for violence done to Negroes has generally resulted in acquittals.

Where a lynching has occurred, the chances of federal prosecution of the lynchers will depend on the circumstances.

—— A mob vested with no authority tracks down a victim and kills him. No federal prosecution is possible.

—— A deputized posse, or one led by a public officer, takes a victim into custody and kills him. Prosecution of all members of the posse is possible under Section 242.

—— A mob takes a victim from the custody of a state officer and kills him, the officer not being involved. No prosecution is possible under Section 242. (If the officer were a federal officer, there is a possibility of prosecution of members of the mob under Section 241).

—— A mob takes a victim from the custody of a state officer and kills him, with the cooperation of the officer. Prosecution of the officer is possible under Section 242. (There is only a doubtful possibility of prosecution of the mob under Section 241).

—— A mob takes a victim from the custody of a state officer and kills him, the officer doing nothing to resist the will of the mob, but not cooperating actively. Prosecution of the Officer for his inaction would appear to be possible under Section 242.

Section 242 can also probably be successfully invoked

60

where there is a willful deprivation on the part of a person acting under the color of law of another individual's right to come and go from one state to another, or to express himself freely, or to worship as he chooses, or of right accruing to an individual under federal laws.

The Right to Vote

All citizens of the United States who are otherwise qualified by law to vote at any election are entitled to vote at all elections, without distinction of race, color or previous condition of servitude. This section, 1971 of Title 42 of the United States Code, was initially passed in 1870, pursuant to the Fifteenth Amendment. It is only recently, however, that it has come to assume potential significance.

For several decades the Supreme Court grappled at various times with the issue of "qualified by law to vote." Even after Court decisions had thrown out as unconstitutional such discriminatory voting provisions as the "grandfather clause," exempting from meeting the standards for voting those whose ancestors fought with the Confederacy, "white primaries" and the attempt to organize the Democratic Party in the South as a private club were all tried in the effort to bar the Negro from the polls. One by one, these efforts legally to circumscribe the Negro's right to vote were stricken down by the Court. But, despite the fact that the Negro's legal right to the franchise has been clearly asserted, he continues to be barred from the polls through a combination of discriminatory literacy tests, fraud, threats and pressure. The need has existed for some type of help to the Negro—and for that matter, any voter—whose right to vote is being interfered with.

To provide such help, Congress enacted the Civil Rights Act of 1957, amended in 1960. To understand this legislation, one must consider yet another civil rights section, 1985 of Title 42 of the United States Code. Section 1985 provides a civil action for damages where a conspiracy of two or more persons exists to deprive a person or a class of persons of their civil rights—specifically, equal protection of the laws, the privileges and immunities of citizens, and the right to vote. The action for damages under this section has never had much meaning. It is important that the Negro's right to vote be protected at the time that an interference takes place, not that he have some illusory right to damages after he has been deprived of the right to vote. Recent federal legislation—known as the Civil Rights Act of 1957 but in fact, an amendment to Section 1985—seeks to accomplish this.

It gives the United States Attorney General the right to come into federal court and ask for an injunction against an official thought to be interfering with the right to vote. If the official persists, the judge may then hold him in civil contempt, and remand him to prison until such time as he is willing to abide by the injunction. Where the judge desires to punish for criminal contempt, he may remand the violating official to prison for not more than 45 days or fine him not more than $1,000 on his own initiative. If he desires to impose more serious punishment, the matter must be tried by a jury.

The original Administration bill sought to provide enforcement through the Attorney General's injunction procedure for all the civil rights covered under Section 1985, but the southern legislators were able to limit this procedure to the right to vote only. Additional features of the Civil Rights Act of 1957 include the creation of a Civil Rights Division in the Attorney General's office to succeed the smaller and inadequate Civil Rights Section, and the authorization of a Commission on Civil Rights to investigate civil rights violations.

The Federal Civil Rights Act of 1960 extends federal protection of voting rights, bars interference with federal court orders, and strengthens federal statutes covering bombings and other forms of violence.

Through the end of 1963, the Department of Justice had filed 45 suits under the Federal Civil Rights Acts of 1957 and 1960, charging denial of voting rights. Federal courts enjoined voter discrimination in numerous counties of the South, and several Supreme Court decisions operated to reinforce the federal powers. Specifically, it ruled that the Federal Civil Rights Commission may subpoena voting registrars and compel testimony without revealing names of Negro complainants; upheld the power of the Attorney General to obtain Alabama voting records in investigating discrimination against Negro voters; affirmed lower court decisions that the Act of 1957 empowers Federal judges to order specific Negroes entered on the voting rolls; and upheld the Department of Justice's demand for Mississippi voting records.

In addition, in 1962, the Congress approved a constitutional amendment outlawing the poll tax as a voting requirement in Federal elections. By the end of 1963, the measure had been ratified by 36 of the 38 states required to make the Amendment effective.

Legislation recently considered and passed by the Congress seeks to further safeguard Negro voting rights, assure equal justice, end segregation in public accommodations, speed school desegregation, spur Negro employment and apprenticeship training, create a Federal Community Relations Service and extend the life of the U. S. Commission on Civil Rights for the third time. (See Appendix).

II. THE STATES AND CIVIL RIGHTS

In 1954, the locus of civil rights legislation—fair employment practices laws, and laws seeking to protect equality of opportunity in education, housing and public accommodations—was in the Northeast—New York, New Jersey, Massachusetts and Connecticut. The South, on the other hand, existed under a massive code of segregation legislation. By 1964, civil rights legislation had moved substantially across the North and West of the country while, as a result of Supreme Court action, substantial inroads had been made on the structure of segregation.

Equal Access to Services and Accommodations

Laws banning racial and religious discrimination in public accommodations now operate in 30 states. While the precise wording and coverage of such laws vary from state to state, in general they protect persons against discrimination on account of religious as well as racial difference; and in most cases, they protect the alien as well as the citizen.

These laws exist in Alaska, California, Colorado, Connecticut, Idaho, Illinoise, Indiana, Iowa, Kansas, Maine, Massachusetts, Maryland, Michigan, Minnesota, Montana, Nebraska, New Hampshire, New Jersey, New Mexico, New York, North Dakota, Ohio, Oregon, Pennsylvania, Rhode Island, South Dakota, Vermont, Washington, Wisconsin and Wyoming. Except for the southern states, whose segregation codes remain on the books, despite the insistent legal attack against them, only Arizona, Nevada and Utah have no legislation protecting against discrimination in public accommodations. The passage of a law in Maryland represents the first such in a southern state.

Many of the public accommodation laws, frequently referred to as "civil rights laws" go back many years in origin, with the result that they provide for enforcement through civil action for damages, or criminal action initiated by the attorney-general's office, or a combination of both. In recent years, it has been realized that administrative, rather than judicial handling of complaints of discrimination, furnishes a more effective remedy. Accordingly, following the earlier lead of Connecticut, Massachusetts, New Jersey, New York and Rhode Island, where an aggrieved party may file complaint with an administrative commission set up to handle all matters of discrimination, Alaska, California, Connecticut, Illinois, Indiana, Kansas, Nebraska, Ohio, Oregon, Pennsylvania and Washington have strengthened their civil rights statutes covering public accommodations.

The following states additionally forbid discriminatory advertising: Colorado, Illinois, Maine, Massachusetts, Michigan, New Hampshire, New Jersey, New York, Pennsylvania, Virginia (religion) and Wisconsin.

SEGREGATION: Laws compelling segregation of the races in all or some of the places of public accommodation or amusement exist in 15 states—Alabama, Arkansas,

Florida, Georgia, Kentucky, Louisiana, Missouri, Mississippi, North Carolina, Oklahoma, South Carolina, Tennessee, Texas, Virginia and West Virginia. The extent to which these laws continue to be enforced is doubtful in many of these states, and is under continuing legal challenge in the others.

For example, in 1963, the Governor of Kentucky issued an executive order barring discrimination in public accommodations, and in El Paso, Texas, a local ordinance has been enacted barring discrimination in public accommodations. In Texas, generally, the practice will vary from city to city and from county to county. In West Virginia and Missouri, without repeal of the segregation laws, there appears to have been voluntary acquiescence in court decisions. Throughout the South, in specific areas and in connection with specific facilities, segregation has been ended by judicial fiat. The following is a partial listing of judicial rulings (Federal courts and Supreme Court) invalidating segregation laws.

—— In a series of cases decided in 1963, involving the states of North Carolina and Louisiana and the City of Birmingham, Ala., the Supreme Court ruled that cities and states with segregation laws or official segregation policies may not prosecute Negroes seeking service in private establishments. This decision would appear to render segregation laws unenforcible, though it must be borne in mind that even with the erosion of the legal structure of segregation, local custom will tend to reenforce patterns of segregation.

—— In a series of cases in the federal courts and at the Supreme Court level, segregation at airports, on trains and buses, in intrastate as well as interstate commerce, and at facilities associated with transportation terminals, is barred, and segregation signs have been ordered removed. In *Bailey* v. *Patterson* (1962), the Supreme Court stated, "we have said beyond question that no state may require racial segregation in interstate or intrastate transportation facilities." It seems apparent, however, that each situation is put to an individual test as southern municipalities and states seek to resist the application of anti-segregation rulings.

—— Wherever public funds, whether state or federal, are involved in a public accommodation, segregation is invalid. Thus segregation at public beaches, on public golf courses, in restaurants operated by government facilities, in public parks and playgrounds, in swimming pools and in recreation facilities in scores of cities throughout the South has been outlawed.

SEGREGATION AND BREACH OF PEACE: Since 1955, with the Montgomery, Ala., bus strike, Negroes and whites alike have utilized so-called "non-violent" social action techniques to break down patterns of segregation. Perhaps the most widespread device has been the "sit-in" at lunch counters in segregated communities to force an end to the refusal to serve Negroes. Communities have reacted by jailing demonstrators for breach of peace.

In 1961, *Garner* v. *Louisiana,* the Supreme Court unanimously voided such a conviction for lack of evidence that the demonstrators had disturbed the peace; and in 1963 (*Edward* v. *South Carolina*) the Court reversed breach of peace convictions of anti-segregation demonstrators in Columbia, S. C., ruling that Negroes had exercised constitutional rights of free speech and assembly "in their most pristine and classic form."

It seems clear that the Court is prepared to invoke the protection of the First Amendment in behalf of civil rights demonstrators, just as freedom of expression was invoked a generation ago to protect the rights of labor to picket.

Equal Opportunity in Employment

FEP LAWS: The broadest protection against discrimination in employment for reasons of race, color or religion is found in Fair Employment Practices legislation (FEP) which regulates private employment and creates an administrative machinery for enforcement. Such legislation now exists in 22 states: Alaska, California, Colorado, Connecticut, Delaware, Hawaii, Illinois, Indiana, Kansas, Massachusetts, Michigan, Minnesota, Missouri, New Jersey, New

Mexico, New York, Ohio, Oregon, Pennsylvania, Rhode Island, Washington and Wisconsin. In addition, Iowa and Vermont have adopted laws making discrimination in employment subject to criminal penalties. At least 41 major municipalities have enacted enforcible fair employment practice ordinances.

HOW FEP WORKS: The following questions and answers based on New York FEP law will serve to describe the basic character and operation of these laws.

What are unlawful employment practices under FEP? (1) for an employer of six or more persons to refuse to employ or to discharge an individual because of race, creed, color or national origin or to discriminate against him in pay or other terms of employment; (2) for a labor organization, because of race, creed, color, or national origin, to exclude or expel an individual from membership or to discriminate against its members, an employer or his employees; (3) for an employer of six or more persons or an employment agency in a statement, advertisement, employment application blank or inquiry to express any requirement as to race, creed, color or national origin; (4) for an employer, a labor organization or employment agency to discriminate against an individual because he has instituted or assisted in any proceeding under the law; (5) for any person to aid, incite, or coerce the doing of any act forbidden by the law.

How is FEP enforced? FEP is generally enforced through a Commission against Discrimination whose members are appointed by the governor. The Commission has the power to receive, investigate and pass on complaints alleging discrimination, to hold hearings and to subpoena witnesses.

What is the procedure of enforcement? An applicant or employee who feels that he has been the victim of an unlawful enployment practice may file a verified complaint with the Commission in which he sets forth the facts. The Commission then makes a prompt investigation through one of its Commissioners, and if it is determined that probable cause exists for believing the unlawful practice by conference, conciliation and persuasion.

If this fails, the Commissioner may order the employer or organization charged to appear at a hearing before three members of the Commission excluding the member who made the investigation. If, at the hearing, the Commission finds that there has been an unlawful employment practice, it will issue an order requiring the offender to cease and desist and to right the wrong which has been committted, i.e. hire the person discriminated against. If no unlawful employment practice is found to have occurred, the complaint is dismissed. Review and enforcement of the Commission's orders is through the courts of the state.

What are the penalties under FEP? Willful violation of an order of the Commission or willfully resisting or impeding the Commission in its attempts to enforce the law is a misdemeanor, punishable by a maximum of one year in prison or a maximum fine of $500 or both.

What groups are exempt from FEP? Social, fraternal, charitable, educational and religious associations—all organizations which are not organized for private profit—are specifically excluded from the law.

What may employers do if their employees refuse to work with persons of particular races or creeds? They may appeal to the Commission for relief, since the law forbids any person, whether employer or employee, to obstruct its enforcement.

Does FEP create a quota system in employment? No, a quota system is an unlawful employment practice under the law.

DISCRIMINATION FORBIDDEN ON PUBLIC WORKS: The following nine states forbid discrimination for reasons of race, color or religion—Arizona, California, Colorado, Massachusetts, Minnesota, New Jersey, New York, Ohio, Pennsylvania. Similar legislation in Illinois, Indiana and Kansas prohibits discrimination on public works specifically for reasons of race or color, but probably embraces religious discrimination as well. Colorado extends the ban on discrimination to all private contractors retained for any work where public tax money is involved, and both Colorado and New York require an anti-discrimination clause to be included in contracts negotiated by the State with contractors. California, by constitutional amendment, now forbids the exclusion of Chinese from employment on public works.

Several States have additional legislation forbidding discrimination in employment on work that is in the public interest. Illinois, Nebraska, New Jersey and New York forbid discrimination in employment in defense work. New York forbids refusal by a public utility company to employ a person because of race, creed, color or national origin. Massachusetts forbids discrimination because of race, color or national origin by street railway companies owned or financially aided by the state. New York, Kansas and Nebraska have specific legislation forbidding discrimination in membership by labor organizations. Discrimination in relief for reasons of race, color or creed is forbidden in Illinois, Massachusetts, New York and Pennsylvania, for reasons of religion by New Jersey and for reasons of color by North Carolina.

It should be borne in mind that in those States where enforcible FEP laws have been enacted, these, in effect, include the narrower legislation dealing with public works, although such legislation remains on the books.

DISCRIMINATION FORBIDDEN IN PUBLIC SERVICE: Religious tests for *public office* are specifically banned in 22 states—Alabama, Arkansas, Georgia, Indiana, Iowa, Kansas, Maine, Maryland, Minnesota, Missouri, Nebraska, New Jersey, Ohio, Oregon, Pennsylvania, Rhode Island, Tennessee, Texas, Utah, Washington, West Virginia, Wisconsin. Actually, under the Constitution, religious tests for public office would be illegal even in the absence of a specific law.

In the area of *civil service*, discrimination for reasons of religion is specifically forbidden in 13 states—California, Connecticut, Kansas, Maine, Massachusetts, Michigan, Minnesota, Nebraska, New Jersey, New York, Ohio, Pennsylvania, Wisconsin. Religious inquiry for civil service positions is forbidden in California, Illinois, Oregon, Pennsylvania and Wisconsin. Discrimination in civil servce employment for reasons of race or color is specifically forbidden in six states which likewise forbid discrimination for reasons of religion—California, Connecticut, Illinois, Massachusetts, Michigan, New York. Michigan also forbids removals from or demotions in civil service for religious or racial reasons. Pennsylvania declares that an employee of the police department may not be removed for religious or racial reasons, and forbids exclusion from examinations for employment in penal or correction institutions because of race or religious opinion.

In the area of *public school appointments,* discrimination for reasons of religion is forbidden in five states—California, Illinois, New Jersey, Wisconsin, Wyoming, and religious inquiry or test for such appointment is forbidden in eight states—California, Colorado, Idaho, Illinois, Iowa, Nebraska, New Mexico, New York. Distrimination in public school appointment for reasons of race or color is forbidden in California, New Jersey ad Wisconsin. New Jersey also provides that dismissals from employment as principal or teacher, resulting from reduction in staff, shall not be based on race or religion.

Equal Opportunity in Education

As of May, 1954, the following states either compelled or expressly permitted segregation—Alabama, Delaware, Florida, Georgia, Kentucky, Louisiana, Maryland, Mississippi, Missouri, New Mexico, North Carolina, Oklahoma, South Carolina, Tennessee, Texas, West Virginia, Wyoming and the District of Columbia. In the famous *School Segregation Cases* (1954, 1955) the Supreme Court ruled compulsory segregation in public schools unconstitutional. School systems were ordered to end segregation "with all deliberate speed" and to move toward integration in a "systematic and effective" manner, within a "reasonable time."

As of October, 1963, New Mexico, Wyoming and Missouri had repealed their school segregation laws, and the District of Columbia had desegregated its public schools. In all but one (Mississippi) of the remaining 14 southern and border states, some 1,141 school districts had made some progress toward desegregation.

Virginia enacted a Pupil Placement Law designed to circumvent desegration, but it was held to be unconstitutional (1957) and Arkansas laws which closed Little Rock high schools were likewise declared unconstitutional (1959). A Louisiana local-option law permitting the closing of public schools as an alternative to integration was held unconstitutional (1962), and a Tennessee law providing for "voluntary" school desegregation was characterized as "patently and manifestly unconstitutional" (1957). In Delaware, a grade-a-year desegregation plan was struck down and full integration ordered for the fall semester (1961).

The degree of resistance to desegregation, from the legal standpoint is perhaps best exemplified by actions in Virginia, all of which were set aside by the inexorable process of court application of the desegregation decision. In 1959, Virginia's State Supreme Court ruled that the state constitution barred closing individual schools in order to thwart desegregation, and in the same year a Federal District Court ruled the "massive resistance" laws unconstitutional. In 1961, the Federal District Court ruled that public funds may not be used to finance private schools for white students of Prince Edward County, as long as public schools were kept closed to avoid integration. A tragic commentary on the Prince Edward situation was the fact that for some three years, Negro youngsters were virtually barred from educational opportunity. In 1962, the Court declared that schools of one county may not be closed to avoid compliance with court orders, while other public schools in the state remain open. And, in 1963, the Supreme Court barred payment of state tuition grants to white private schools pending the Court's review of the Prince Edward school closing case. Elsewhere in the deep South, resistance frequently took the form of violence and terror, as distinguished from Virginia's effort to utilize legal measures to avoid desegregation.

Nor was the North without its problems in this area.

71

While 11 states forbid exclusion of or discrimination against students in public schools for reasons of race or color, and court action operates to invalidate segregation of students everywhere, the emerging fact of the "neighborhood school" has created de facto segregation even where integration, as a matter of law, is not resisted. This has resulted in a legal focus on segregation in northern schools. An initial confrontation took place in New Rochelle where a lower court order requiring the city to desegregate a gerrymandered, predominantly Negro school was affirmed by the Supreme Court. A similar legal battle was launched in Englewood, New Jersey.

In New York State, the State Education Commissioner ordered a racial census of all public schools in 1961 in a drive to eliminate de facto segregation. In 1963, this was followed up by an order to all school boards to take steps to correct racial imbalance in the public schools. In an initial test of the Commissioner's authority in Malverne, Long Island, a lower court refused to sustain the Commisioner's power.

Many northern school districts have become involved in the demands and counter-demands relating to the bussing or transferring of students out of their neighborhoods in order to end de facto segregation. White parents have demonstrated, claiming that the civil rights of their children are infringed by programs designed to take children out of their neighborhoods in order to create integrated schools. Court battles on so-called "forced integration" are shaping up in variety of northern metropolitan communities.

At the college level, state colleges fall within the Supreme Court's invalidation of "separate but equal" facilities As a result, the laws requiring separate colleges for whites and Negroes, while still on the books of some 15 states, are rendered null and void. While desegregation at the college level was accomplished in the Middle South with a minimum of organized resistance, the attempts to desegregate state universities in Alabama and Mississippi created national issues as the governors of both of these states set their own authority against that of the federal government. Both states, however, finally yielded to federal authority, and in the face of citations for contempt and the threat of fines and prison sentences, the governors deferred.

At the same time, laws forbidding discrimination for reasons of race, color or creed in private colleges have now been enacted in six states—Connecticut, Idaho, Massachusetts, New Jersey, New York and Pennsylvania. Similar in conception to FEP laws, these laws are known as Fair Educational Practices Laws, and, in effect, they are designed to bar the use of the "quota system" in governing the entry of minority group students into private colleges. Enforcement is through hearings and the issuance of cease and desist orders, and in general, the state commissions set up under FEP have been given jurisdiction and authority over the administration of Fair Educational Practices laws.

Equal Opportunity in Housing

PUBLIC HOUSING: Discrimination for race, creed or color is now forbidden in 13 states—Alaska, California, Colorado, Connecticut, Indiana, Massachusetts, Minnesota, New Hampshire, New Jersey, New York, Oregon, Pennsylvania and Wisconsin.

PUBLICLY ASSISTED HOUSING: Discrimination for race, creed or color is now forbidden in 9 states—Alaska, California, Colorado, Connecticut, Massachusetts, New Jersey, New York, Oregon and Pennsylvania.

URBAN RENEWAL: Redevelopment housing—the replacement of a slum area with a newly planned community—is closely associated with publicly assisted housing. California, Colorado, Illinois, Massachusetts, Minnesota, Montana, New Jersey, New York, and Pennsylvania all forbid discrimination in the selection of tenants for renewal projects.

MORTGAGE LENDERS: Colorado, Connecticut, Massachusetts, Minnesota, New Jersey, New York and Pennsylvania—a total of 7 states bar discrimination by mortgage lenders.

PRIVATE HOUSING: Fair Housing Practices laws—

again, in the mould of FEP—have been enacted in 11 states —Alaska, California, Colorado, Connecticut, Massachusetts, Minnesota, New Hampshire, New Jersey, New York, Oregon and Pennsylvania. In Connecticut, Massachusetts, and New York, the only exemptions are owner-occupied one- or two-family dwellings. The Supreme Court has upheld constitutionality by refusing to review.

The City of New York in 1957 adopted the first ordinance in the country barring racial or religious discrimination in private housing. In 1961, the ordinance was broadened to include 95% of all dwellings. Enforcement is simplified. The Commission on Human Rights is authorized to seek restraining order barring disposal of property pending outcome of proceedings. The cities of Philadelphia, Pittsburgh, Schenectady, N.Y. and Albuquerque, N.M. have since followed suit.

RESTRICTIVE COVENANTS: The racial restrictive covenants in a deed or lease by which land cannot be sold or leased to persons of particular religious or racial groups was declared unenforcible by the Supreme Court in 1948. California (1961) and New York (1962) enacted legislation voiding racial and ethnic restrictive covenants in real property deeds, and Minnesota has had such a statute on its books since 1919.

REGULATION OF REAL ESTATE BROKERS: The Connecticut Commission on Civil Rights, the Attorneys-General of California, Massachusetts and Oregon, and the Superior Court of Washington, have ruled that real estate brokers are covered by state laws barring discrimination in services offered to the public. Real estate licensing authorities in New York and Pennsylvania have barred racial or religious discrimination by real estate salesmen and brokers in sales or rentals and forbid efforts to stimulate panic selling in real estate transactions.

Equal Opportunity to Health and Welfare Service

New Jersey and New York have laws dealing with the problem of discrimination in health and welfare services, although it would appear that any such facility which is either publicly maintained or publicly assisted would fall within the requirement that administration must be on a non-discriminatory basis, else constitutional rights are violated. New Jersey forbids discrimination for reasons of race, creed, color, national origin or ancestry in the admission of disabled or indigent sick to city hospitals. Both states, in their public accommodation laws, include clinics, dispensaries and hospitals in the enumeration of public accommodations in which discrimination for race, color or creed is forbidden.

Among the southern states, segregation in hospitals and welfare institutions is the general rule, and to date, there has not yet been a concerted legal attack on these practices, although the indications are clear that it is only a matter of time before every aspect of the structure of segregation will have come under legal scrutiny and will have been found to be a violation of "civil rights."

Chapter Four

SEPARATION OF CHURCH AND STATE

The principle of separation of Church and State is found in the First Amendment to the Constitution:

"Congress shall make no law respecting an establishment of religion, or prohibiting the free exercise thereof. . ."

After the passage of the 14th Amendment, the courts held that the states, as well as the Federal government were bound by this provision.

Clearly an assertion of freedom of religion, a classic question which, in the last fifteen years has become a social and legal issue, relates to the intent of the First Amendment with regard to the relationship between Church and State. Nor has this issue been an academic one. For it involves such matters as the permissibility of Bible reading and the recital of the Lord's Prayer in schools; release of youngsters from school to attend religious education; use of school premises by religious groups; fringe benefit assistance to students in attendance at parochial schools; and a host of related issues.

As in most of the areas of civil liberty and civil rights, it has been the Supreme Court which has defined and articulated the basic principle—namely, that in the words of Thomas Jefferson, the First Amendment clause was intended to erect "a wall of separation between Church and State." The rule was laid down in 1947 in a case (*Everson v. Board of Education*) which involved free bus transportation to children attending parochial schools. While the provision for the bus transportation was upheld, the broad principle of law enunciated had sweeping significance. The language of the Court is instructive:

"Neither a state nor the Federal Government can set up a Church.

Neither can pass laws which aid one religion, aid all religions, or prefer one religion over another.

Neither can force nor influence a person to go or to remain away from church against his will or force him to profess a belief or disbelief in any religion.

No person can be punished for entertaining or professing religious beliefs or disbeliefs, for church attendance or nonattendance.

No tax in any amount, large or small, can be levied to support any religious activities or institutions, whatever they may be called, or whatever form they may adopt to teach or practice religion.

Neither a state nor the Federal Government can, openly or secretly, participate in the affairs of any religious organizations or groups and vice versa."

The application of these principles does not occur in a vacuum. The result has been public controversy sometimes as bitter, if not more overtly bitter, than the controversy raging over desegregation. Since most of the issues appear to relate to the schools, the controversy has ranged over the gamut of public education. In a welter of charges and counter-charges, those asserting the strict principle of separation have been accused of a desire to secularize the schools and to drive God from public American life. The strict separationists, on the other hand, protest that the church and the home bear the responsibility for religious education, and that it is an affirmation of the role of religion in American life to underscore that responsibility lies outside of government.

Against this background, the current state of the law may be reviewed.

I. RELIGION AND THE SCHOOLS

Prayers and Bible Reading

Few judicial decisions have produced more violent controversy than the Supreme Court's ruling in the Regents' Prayer case (*Engel v. Vitale*).

On June 25, 1962, the Court held 6-1 that the 22-word prayer adopted by the New York State Board of Regents in 1951 was "wholly inconsistent with the Establishment Clause" of the First Amendment. The prayer read: "Almighty God, we acknowledge our dependence upon Thee, and we beg Thy blessing upon us, our parents, our teachers and our country."

Writing for the majority, Justice Hugo L. Black, said:

". . . The First Amendment was added to the Constitution . . . as a guarantee that neither the power nor the prestige of the Federal Government would be used to control, support or influence the kinds of prayer the American people can say. . . . It is no part of the business of government to compose official prayers for any group . . . to recite as part of a religious program carried on by the government. . . . Neither the fact that the prayer may be denominationally neutral, nor . . . that its observance . . . is voluntary can serve to free it from the limitations of the Establishment Clause. . . . It is neither sacrilegious nor antireligious to say that each separate government in this country should stay out of the business of writing or sanctioning official prayers and leave that purely religious function to the people themselves and to those the people choose to look to for religious guidance."

The *Engel* case dealt with a prayer, however innocuous, prepared and sponsored by governmental authority. One year later, however, on June 17, 1963, the Supreme Court rendered an even more far-reaching decision. The Court held, 8-1, that Pennsylvania's Bible-reading statute and Baltimore's rule requiring the recitation of the Lord's Prayer or the reading of the Bible at the opening of the public school day were unconstitutional under the Establishment Clause of the First Amendment. In neither case was attendance at the school exercises compulsory. Justice Clark concluded for the majority as follows:

"The place of religion in our society is an exalted one, achieved through a long tradition of reliance on the home, the church and the inviolable citadel of the individual heart and mind. We have come to recognize through bitter experience that it is not within the power of government to invade that citadel. . . . In the relationship between man and religion, the state is firmly committed to a position of neutrality."

So divided has been the reaction of the public, the leaders of the faiths and opinion moulders that a constitutional amendment has been introduced, designed to overturn the Supreme Court decision. The text of the Becker Amendment is as follows:

Section 1. Nothing in this Contsitution shall be deemed to prohibit the offering, reading from, or listening to prayers or biblical scriptures, if participation therein is on a voluntary basis, in any governmental or public school, institution or place.

Section 2. Nothing in this Constitution shall be deemed to prohibit making reference to belief in, reliance upon, or invoking the aid of, God or a Supreme Being, in any governmental or public document, proceeding, activity, ceremony, school, institution or place or upon any coinage, currency, or obligation of the United States.

Section 3. Nothing in this article shall constitute an establishment of religion.

Thus far, there has been no marked progress toward moving the Amendment through Congress.

Released Time

Within four decades, all but two of the fifty states have put "released time" programs into operation. Under these programs, children are excused from school, with the consent of their parents in order to receive religious instruction. It is estimated that some 27 million public school children in about 3,000 communities are presently enrolled in these programs.

In 1948, the Supreme Court held (*McCollum v. Board of Education*) that such classes may not constitutionally be held on school premises. But in 1952, when confronted with the factual situation of released time classes conducted off school premises and without pressure on youngsters to participate, the Court held such practices valid under the First Amendment. (*Zorach v. Clauson*).

The related problem of the use of school premises by religious groups has not been confronted in court. The plain fact is that all religious groups at one point or another have been beneficiaries of communal sentiment in favor of opening the school doors to pressed parishes and congregations or where emergencies are involved. While issues are formulated in the legal and constitutional arena, the public generally and frequently crosses the "wall of separation."

Religious Holiday Observances

Severe community tensions have been engendered where the issue of Christmas observance in the schools has been raised. Generally, where such observances have been traditional in preponderantly Christian communities, the objection of newer Jewish residents has touched off conflict. Thus far, however, there has been no articulate attempt to have the matter resolved legally.

The spectrum of opinion ranges from those who would perpetuate the established tradition, including the celebration of the Nativity itself. Others favor the screening of such observances to eliminate purely doctrinal aspects, including the Nativity. Still others suggest the introduction of Hanukah observance as a type of balance to the Christmas observance. At the far end of the spectrum are those who feel that religious holiday observances of any faith are outside the purview of the school and a violation of the First Amendment.

Whether the Supreme Court decisions on matters of Bible reading and prayers in the schools will lead inevitably to a test of the legality of religious holiday observances remains to be seen.

Government Aid to Education

Yet another aspect of the overall issue of religion and the schools is the degree to which government assistance may be rendered to students of parochial institutions. Opponents of such aid take the position that, in essence, this is aid to a religious or religiously-sponsored institution. Those who favor such aid point out that the benefit is for the student and his family and that the aid afforded the institution thereby is incidental. The law, as well as public opinion, is fairly split.

BUS TRANSPORTATION: In 1947, the Supreme Court decided (*Everson v. Board of Education*) that it was not unconstitutional for the State of New Jersey to furnish bus transportation to children in attendance at parochial schools under the same terms and conditions as such transpartation was furnished to public school students. The service was characterized as a "welfare benefit" for students.

At least seven states have affirmatively held to the contrary under their state constitutions. These are: Alaska, Maine, Missouri, New Mexico, Oklahoma, Washington and Wisconsin. Pennsylvania, in 1963, defeated a bill providing for tax-paid bus transportation in behalf of parochial school children. In Ohio, the Attorney-General ruled that no authority existed for bus transportation to be furnished to students at private and parochial schools, but indicated that legislation providing such authority would be constitutional.

TEXTBOOKS: As early as 1930 (*Cochran v. Louisiana State Board of Education*) the Supreme Court held that it was constitutional for the states to enact statutes providing free textbooks for children in non-public schools. Yet, only four states—Louisiana, Mississippi, Rhode Island and West Virginia—now supply textbook aid for non-public schools. Seven other states which had previously provided such aid have since invalidated it.

FEDERAL AID: In a special message to Congress in January 1963 President John F. Kennedy offered a comprehensive plan to provide funds for education from elementary through graduate school. A bill designed to carry out this program (H. R. 3000, described as the National Improvement Act of 1963) included aids for church-related as well as public educational institutions. In higher education, particularly, church-related schools were to be made eligible for massive aid: construction loans for academic facilities; loans and grants for the construction of library

81

facilities and for books; grants for the expansion of graduate schools, applicable to construction, faculty, and equipment; increased appropriations for foreign-language studies; expansion of the scope of teacher institutes, and grants to strengthen the preparation of elementary-and secondary-school teachers and teachers of gifted, handicapped, and retarded children. In addition, there were provisions for loans, work-study programs, and graduate fellowships for students in church-related colleges. Among the provisions for elementary and secondary education, the bill extended the National Defense Education Act, which provided loans to parochial and other non-public schools for science, mathematics, and foreign-language teaching equipment.

In February the House Education and Labor Committee began hearing on the bill. It soon became clear that the higher-education features would have fairly clear sailing. In May the administration abandoned its comprehensive aid-to-education bill in favor of separate measures, and in August the House passed a college-aid bill, which included aid to church-related colleges. It overwhelmingly rejected an amendment which would have paved the way for judicial review of the church-state aspects of the measures.

In the Senate, Winston L. Prouty (Rep., Vt.) and Wayne Morse (Dem., Ore.) clashed over the constitutionality of grants, as distinguished from loans, to church-related colleges. Prouty favored grants and loans for construction purposes, calling it "patently absurd" to question the constitutionality of aiding the construction of science classrooms in church-related colleges. Morse, on the other hand, thought the church-related college should be excluded from tax-raised grants because it exercises a religious influence over its students, but that loans would not violate the First Amendment "if the interest covers the cost of the use of the money." Sam J. Ervin (Dem., N.C.) questioned the constitutionality of both loans and grants to church-controlled colleges and universities and offered an amendment for judicial review which was included in the bill adopted by the Senate.

In November a House-Senate conference committee

reached agreement on a bill, the Senate conferees yielding on the judicial-review section. Grants were for "academic facilities," especially "designed for instruction or research in the natural or physical sciences, mathematics, modern foreign languages, or engineering, or for use as a library" and not "for sectarian instruction or . . . religious worship." The bill provided that if its conditions for the use of facilities were met, such facilities would become the property of the private institution after a period of 20 years. It authorized an expenditure of $1.195 billion for the first three years of a five-year program and provided for a re-examination of the program before funds were authorized for the remaining two years. In November the House approved the conference committee report, 258-92, and in mid-December the Senate approved, 54-27. In signing the measure into law in December, 1963, President Lyndon B. Johnson called it the most significant education bill in history, the first broad assistance program for colleges since the Land Grant Act a century earlier.

The New York *Times* applauded the "great advance" represented by the college-aid bill, but regretted the "blurring of the lines of separation of church and state. The pragmatic compromise that took final form in the bill evolved from the almost insoluble mixtures of various degrees of church-relatedness in different colleges. What matters now is that the compromise be regarded as an unfortunate, if perhaps necessary, step under the special circumstances of America's peculiar higher education system—and not as a foot in the door."

The Paradoxes

Notwithstanding what appears to be increasing restriction by judicial fiat on the admixture of religious and secular activities, in other areas, there appears to be relatively little challenge. Thus, the tax exempt status of religious institutions appears quite secure, and recent tax legislation has, in fact, liberalized deductions taken for contributions to such institutions. Apparently, there is a distinction as to what it is appropriate to do with the tax dollar once collected as distinguished from the basis of exempting it from collection in the first place.

Similarly seemingly inconsistent are such widely varied practices as the impression on coins of "In God we Trust," the mention of the deity in the pledge of allegiance, provision for chaplains in the Armed Forces, clergymen in service at sessions of Congress, presidential proclamations on Thanksgiving day and a host of other evidences that there is acknowledgment of a Supreme Being. Perhaps, the test is simply that, in the schools, where the setting is one of indoctrination, the religious objective has no place.

II. OTHER FIRST AMENDMENT ISSUES

To some extent, the issue of "freedom from religion" has tended to obscure that of "freedom of religion." But since the days of Roger Williams, the country has progressed increasingly toward acceptance of the minority point of view as dictated by religious conscience.

While, in general, the law follows the prescript that "we render to Caesar the things that are Caesar's," governmental tolerance of non-conformity based in religious conviction has broadened. Thus, while in 1940 (*Minersville v. Gobitis*) the power of the state to require the flag salute in public schools was upheld against the assertion by a family of Jehovah's Witnesses that this ceremony was contrary to their religious belief, three years later, (*West Virginia v. Barnette*) the Court reversed itself and came to the opposite conclusion. (See above, p. 25)

In like manner, the treatment in World War II of "conscientious objectors" was far more sympathetic than it had been in World War 1. However, religious belief has not been permitted to justify polygamy. Inversely, the jurisdiction of the state over public education is not so broad or inclusive as to permit a state to render a parochial school system illegal.

A legal paradox was created in connection with the issue of the entitlement to unemployment benefits of a person whose religious convictions keep him from accepting employment requiring work on Saturday.

While the Court decided (*Sherbert v. Verner*) on the same day that it ruled Bible reading and the Lord's Prayer recitation invalid that the Government had no right to impose a choice which puts a burden on the free exercise of religion, the question arises whether unemployment benefits, representing tax moneys, when paid to a person whose entitlement stems from pursuit of certain religious beliefs, is not in effect an assistance to religion. Justice Stewart, the perennial dissenter in the prayer cases, and perhaps with judicial tongue in cheek, stated the proposition:

> "If Mrs. Sherbert's refusal to work on Saturday were based on indolence, no one would argue that she was not available for work. But because her refusal . . . was based upon her religious creed, the Establishment Clause requires that she be paid unemployment compensation benefits, thus requiring financial support of government to be placed behind a particular religious belief."

Perhaps a more practical paradox is the clearcut inconsistency of this decision with the 1961 upholding of Sunday closing-laws (*Braunfeld v. Brown*). Both cases involved the issue of choice between livelihood and religion. Justices Harlan and White took the position that the *Sherbert* decision overruled *Braunfeld,* but they were a concurring majority only.

An analogous issue involved the vacation of conviction of one, Mrs. Owen Jenison, who had been sentenced by a lower Minnesota court to 30 days in jail for refusing to take a juror's oath, which she alleged, was "against her Bible." The *Sherbert* holding was regarded as controlling.

On the issue of closing laws, New York State has now enacted an option to the City of New York to exempt Saturday observers fromthe provisions of the state's Sunday closing statute. The measure was limited to family businesses only. Exercising the option, the City Council enacted an ordinance in implementation. Thus was brought to final, although only partial, fruition a long struggle to bring relief from the strictures of the state's closing law to the largest Jewish community in the world.

APPENDIX

Analysis of the

Federal Civil Rights Act of 1964

The long debated civil rights bill is substantially the same as one adopted earlier by the House of Representatives. The principal amendment added by the Senate deals with enforcement procedure in the fair employment and public accommodations sections. In these sections, the Senate bill delays Federal intervention until state and local authorities have a chance to obtain voluntary compliance.

Here, in summary, are the main provisions of the final Senate bill:

Title I — Voting

Prohibits registrars from applying different standards to white and Negro voting applicants and from disqualifying applicants because of inconsequential errors on their forms. Requires that literacy tests be in writing, except under special arrangements for blind persons, and that any applicant desiring one be given a copy of the questions and his answers. Makes a sixth-grade education a rebuttable presumption of literacy. Allows the Attorney General or defendant state officials in any voting suit to request trial by a three-judge Federal Court.

Title II — Public Accommodations

Prohibits discrimination or refusal of service on account of race in hotels, motels, restaurants, gasoline stations and places of amusement if their operations affect interstate commerce or if their discrimination "is supported by state action." Permits the Attorney General to enforce the title by suit in the Federal courts if he believes that any person or group is engaging in a "pattern or practice of resistance" to the rights declared by the title. The latter language was added in the Senate, which also authorized three-judge courts for suits under this title.

Title III — Public Facilities

Requires that Negroes have equal access to, and treatment in, publicly owned or operated facilities such as parks, stadiums and swimming pools. Authorizes the Attorney General to sue for enforcement of these rights if private citizens are unable to sue effectively.

Title IV — Public Schools

Empowers the Attorney General to bring school desegregation suits under the same conditions as in Title III. Authorizes technical and financial aid to school districts to assist in desegregation. The Senate strengthened a provision in the House bill saying that the title does not cover busing of pupils or other steps to end "racial imbalance."

Title V — Civil Rights Commission

Extends the life of the Civil Rights Commission until Jan. 13, 1968.

Title VI — Federal Aid

Provides that no person shall be subjected to racial discrimination in any program receiving Federal aid. Directs Federal agencies to take steps against discrimination, including —as a last resort, and after hearings—withholding of Federal funds from state or local agencies that discriminate.

Title VII — Employment

Bans discrimination by employers or unions with 100 or more employes or members the first year the act is effective, reducing over four years to 25 or more. Establishes a commission to investigate alleged discrimination and use persuasion to end it. Authorizes the Attorney General to sue if he believes any person or group is engaged in a "pattern or practice" of resistance to the title, and to ask for trial by a three-judge court. The Senate added the "pattern-or-practice" condition and shifted the power to sue from the commission to the Attorney General.

Title VIII — Statistics

Directs the Census Bureau to compile statistics of registration and voting by race in areas of the country designated by the Civil Rights Commission. This might be used to enforce the long-forgotten provision of the 14th Amendment that states that discriminate in voting shall lose seats in the House of Representatives.

Title IX — Courts

Permits appellate review of decisions by Federal District judges to send back to the state courts criminal defendants who have attempted to remove their cases on the ground that their civil rights would be denied in state trials. Permits the Attorney General to intervene in suits filed by private persons complaining that they have been denied the equal protection of the laws.

Title X — Conciliation

Establishes a Community Relations Service in the Commerce Department to help conciliate racial disputes. The Senate removed a House ceiling of seven employes.

Title XI — Miscellaneous

Guarantees jury trials for criminal contempt under any part of the act but Title I—a provision added in the Senate. Provides that the statute shall not invalidate state laws with consistent purposes, and that it shall not impair any existing powers of Federal officials.

INDEX

INDEX (Continued)

16-401